The Author

Andrew Thorburn grew up on a small farm near Bridport, obtained a degree in physical Geography, served two years in the Royal Navy, married, and taught himself town and country planning. He worked as a planner for five different County Councils with an interlude directing the Notts-Derbys. Sub-regional Study. Andrew is the father of three children. He has written many papers on the policies and processes of town planning and a book entitled "Planning Villages" published by Estates Gazette in 1971.

During nine years as County Planning Officer of East Sussex he served as President of the Royal Town Planning Institute and initiated the foundation of the Sussex Heritage Trust. In 1983 he was appointed Chief Executive of the English Tourist Board. Two years later he resigned to work in tourism and leisure consultancy, first with Pannell Kerr Forster, then Grant Thornton, and finally with his own firm, which continues. He wrote this book whilst cruising in a small yacht in the Mediterranean.

THE MISSING MUSEUM

Andrew Thorburn

TRAFFORD

© Copyright 2006 Andrew Thorburn.
All rights reserved. No part of this publication may be reproduced, stored in a retrieval system, or transmitted, in any form or by any means, electronic, mechanical, photocopying, recording, or otherwise, without the written prior permission of the author.

Note for Librarians: A cataloguing record for this book is available from Library and Archives Canada at www.collectionscanada.ca/amicus/index-e.html
ISBN 1-4120-8678-7

Printed in Victoria, BC, Canada. Printed on paper with minimum 30% recycled fibre.
Trafford's print shop runs on "green energy" from solar, wind and other environmentally-friendly power sources.

TRAFFORD
PUBLISHING™

Offices in Canada, USA, Ireland and UK

Book sales for North America and international:
Trafford Publishing, 6E–2333 Government St.,
Victoria, BC V8T 4P4 CANADA
phone 250 383 6864 (toll-free 1 888 232 4444)
fax 250 383 6804; email to orders@trafford.com

Book sales in Europe:
Trafford Publishing (UK) Limited, 9 Park End Street, 2nd Floor
Oxford, UK OX1 1HH UNITED KINGDOM
phone 44 (0)1865 722 113 (local rate 0845 230 9601)
facsimile 44 (0)1865 722 868; info.uk@trafford.com

Order online at:
trafford.com/06-0434

10 9 8 7 6 5 4 3 2

This book is dedicated to those who supported and helped us in our endeavour.

CONTENTS

Introduction		1
1.	The beginning	5
2.	Demand and supply	13
3.	We needed some numbers	18
4.	Our selection	25
5.	Raising the money	35
6.	The legal contracts	40
7.	London's communities	44
8.	The customers	51
9.	The Police perspective	57
10.	How policing has changed	67
11.	Policemen in Bow Street	71
12.	The museum concept	78
13.	What shall we call it?	80
14.	SMUCHII	84
15.	Choosing the team	89
16.	Commissioning the design and fit-out	96
17.	Aspirations	106
18.	The design briefs for the Features	111
19.	The rest of the content	150
20.	The virtual museum	154
21.	Adapting the premises	159
22.	The Magistrates Next door	173
23.	Un-cooperative planners	176
24.	Abandonment	185
25.	Plod's law	190
Index		198

Text inserts
  The advertisement   4
  Table of visitor numbers - London attractions   16
  The Blue Lamps tourist leaflet   27
  Problems and solutions   31
  Key elements of our proposal   34
  Black Christian Civic Forum leaflet   48
  The ten messages with police comments   61
  Statement of our common purpose and values   65
  The features lists   100
  "A constable at Bow Street"   104
  The professional advisors   172
Pictures and plans
  The former Bow Street Police Station   cover
  The site   12
  The main entrance for visitors   17
  The proposed museum interior (sketches)   24 and 26
  The first model of the proposal   29
  Ground floor plan for first proposal   30
  Police Station and Courts when new   70
  Building ground floor layout when new   74
  Award winning policemen about 1906   76
  The logo for the museum   83
  The team   94
  The museum shop (sketch)   153
  Policemen's leisure activities at Bow Street   158
  The side wall of the property   160
  The rear wall facing the service yard   161
  Diagram showing environmental analysis   163
  Pictures of model of the proposed building   164, 165, 166
  Full front façade   171
  Proposed ground floor plan and landscaping   180
  The gap between the old and new buildings   184

Introduction

My story begins in 1997 when the two police forces that look after London came together to find a private firm that would create, finance, and run a police museum. They wanted a modern interactive and essentially educational experience particularly attractive to younger people. The former police station at Bow Street, Covent Garden, was available to lease. It was going to be a popular and high profile scheme because of its historic Central London location and heavyweight official support.

The consortium that I put together to develop and run the museum was selected by the Police as its "private sector partner". They agreed to lease us the property, to endorse and help market the museum, to provide us with exhibits and give us access to historical material and their expert advice on policing. We invited the Police to become shareholders with us in the enterprise but they were unable to take any commercial risks.

Over the next four years our team carefully planned every aspect of the project, raised the finance and obtained planning permission, solving numerous problems as we went along. All seemed set for work to start on site when in 2003 the Metropolitan Police Authority wrote to say that they would be acting illegally if they continued with the museum despite the contracts that had been signed. The Authority has now sold the property and thereby ended the 265-year association of Bow Street with good policing. The museum has gone missing.

Developers rarely write descriptions of their work. This may be because deals have to remain confidential or a clear account might harm others, or just a lack of motive. The consequence of this absence of books and articles about the processes of development is that most people on the fringe of the activity have very little knowledge and many misconceptions about what is involved. This includes journalists, planners, bankers, councillors, environmental lobbyists, leisure managers and nascent property entrepreneurs. This was why, when I was working on the project, I decided to write a book afterwards. It could be sold to visitors who had seen the museum.

After the project was stopped it was more important to publish our blueprint for the museum. This is not as interesting as visiting the museum, but it offers some chance of not wasting our team's ideas. Perhaps it will help those with similar projects in mind. In addition, an explanation of how we arrived at the blueprint might serve my original purpose. Most people learn readily from the experiences of others.

Readers will want to know why the museum was not implemented and in the last two chapters there is an account of what happened. Some lessons for developers and public authorities can be drawn from this and I hope that by telling the story I shall help to avoid anything like it happening again.

When I started this project I knew almost nothing about police work and had no personal connections with people who provide police services. My professional experience and interests are in town planning, tourism development and operations, business planning and local government. The project would not be difficult to achieve. But no-body knew then that the Police could and would stop the project much further along the way.

It was with this background that I looked forward to achieving an attractive museum and conserving the building, but most of all my heart is in trying to make places better. A police museum for London would make its policing easier and more effective. This would add to its prosperity and social harmony. Looking back over two hundred years, London could not have become so successful without the quality of policing it has enjoyed. Looking forward into the twenty-first century we should celebrate, continue and enhance these benefits. The museum was to have been one way of doing this.

The effect upon London of not completing the missing museum is to me a tragedy far more damaging than the waste of effort, time and money, which were the most obvious consequences of untimely abandonment by one of the Authorities. The City of London Police remained supportive to the end.

Responsibility for the book is personal and has not been shared with anyone else. To be unrestrained in my comments, II chose not to ask our development partners Salmon Harvester, or the police's project co-ordinator Alan Moss, to help with its writing or review any draft

My thanks to Jestico and Whiles, Alan Moss and London Police Education Ltd. for allowing me to use their written material, drawings and illustrations to make it more interesting.

The book would not have been written without all the work that was done on the project and this is my opportunity to thank all those who contributed, including the following people.

Alan Moss, who served as the indefatigable consultant and company secretary to London Police Education Ltd., which is the charity the police set up to take forward the project. He handled nearly all of the liaison between the Police and our consortium. He has an excellent knowledge of police history and an untiring enthusiasm for the project. It was really his idea in the first place and he is missing the museum more than anyone.

INTRODUCTION

The City of London Police Service always supported us. Its practical assistance came through Peter Gehnich, who seemed keen on the project and was always helpful when called upon.

Will Baker is an engineer with imaginative ideas and an extraordinary and ever growing network of contacts. He became the co-director of Bow Street Partners Ltd. the firm that I set up to take the project forward and without his enthusiasm, countless ideas and wise counsel we would not have gone so far.

Tom Tinner of Mowlem helped us enthusiastically whilst we were tendering. I am sure that this would have gone on had not his firm had second thoughts about its role in the project.

Paul Stoodley was the development director of Salmon Harvester and once that Company had decided to finance and convert the property he put enormous effort into sorting out the problems and making it happen. His good humour, thoroughness and clarity of view were most appreciated.

Tony Ingram is a director of Jestico and Whiles**Error! Bookmark not defined.**, the architects I chose because they seemed to be good at this kind of work. He was always enthusiastic for the project and ably drove it forward. His vision of the way in which the conversion of the building could be carried out was exemplary and he was always at the helm when needed.

Our negotiations with Heritage Projects as prospective operators introduced us to the knowledge and timely guidance of David Lang, Juliana Delaney, and Mark Sandberg who were ever helpful and cheerful.

Neil Holmes was briefed to find the finance and did so successfully. He did more than this, being most positive, thoughtful, inventive and cheerful whenever we spoke about our problems.

We were helped by many specialist professionals, especially Julian Ravest, Simon Harris, Daniel Lister, Erik Dinandt, Ian Russell, Thomas Lisle, Sharon Feldman, Michael Hobson, Alastair Dryburgh, Nick Ferenczy, James Tatham, Sarah Byfield, Mike Howie, John Stevenson, Catherine Morris, Bob Melling, Sam Burford, Lance Bohl, Yomi Falana, Pat Gill, Andrew Lawrence, Mark van den Berg, David Rolton, Peter Rolton, Andrew Cunnington, David Clarke Steve Kuntze, David Baird, Myles Bridges, and Julian Hind. The list would be incomplete without mentioning Graham Douglas and Philip Fletcher who patiently carried forward the key property negotiations. I wholeheartedly thank them all for their stimulus, ideas, expertise and commitment.

AndrewThorburn
March 2006

TENDERS

LONDON POLICE MUSEUM

The Metropolitan Police Service, on behalf of London Police Education Ltd, a registered charity, is seeking partner(s) for a Private Finance Initiative solution to finance, design, build and operate a London Police museum using the former Bow Street Police Station, 28 Bow Street, Covent Garden, London, WC2.

The aim of the museum is to use the police station as a major educational and heritage attraction to educate and entertain the public, and young people in particular, about the role of police and policing issues in London. The museum will contain many of the items of historical interest owned by the Metropolitan Police Service and the City of London Police, and will use modern exhibition techniques.

The Police Service will retain control over the overall style, content and ethos of the museum, but wish to work with partner(s) at the earliest opportunity in the development and planning process. It is anticipated that an application to the Heritage Lottery Fund will be made.

An advertisement has been posted in the Official Journal of the European Communities, a copy of which is available on request.

Expressions of interest should be made no later than 12th February 1998, to the address shown below, stating clearly the range of services being offered, the level of investment which might be considered (if possible) and the extent of willingness to work with others.

Further details may be obtained from:
Department of Procurement and Commercial Services
Second floor, Ocean Block, Cobalt Square
1 South Lambeth Road, London SW8 1SU
Telephone: 0171 230 8643. Fax: 0171 230 8229

1
The beginning

Sitting before my log fire during the (1997) post-Christmas lull, I turned the back page of Leisure Week and came across an advertisement (opposite). When I had read it and read it again I felt a surge of adrenalin, for here was an interesting opportunity that well suited me.

The Metropolitan Police wanted someone to design, build, operate and finance a police museum for London. It would be in Bow Street, which is famous for its Magistrates Court and the Bow Street Runners who are known as the first police force in England - and it was directly opposite the Royal Opera House. What a good location! The advertisement, and its sister in the Official Journal of the European Community was placed on behalf of London Police Education Ltd., an educational charity set up to implement the project.

This was exciting. Here was the chance to create a first class visitor attraction all about a good human interest subject that most people like to hear about. What did we need? I thought that what we needed was a good concept for a visitor attraction, plus planning permission, money, a design team, an operating team and the lease of the former Police Station. Well, with Police support I could fix all that easily enough. Could I get the job? In my business the chance of obtaining a project that is publicly advertised is less than one in five. It was worth a try, but hold back on the excitement – if you can!

The museum was going to have the authenticity provided by the endorsement of the two London police forces. The Metropolitan Police was set up in 1829 and is the largest police force in Britain with about 26,000 officers. The City of London Police with one square mile to look after has about 2,000 officers, a different character and a much longer history. My colleagues and I all thought that our business risks would be relatively low with this project because we could not have a more trustworthy partner in the venture than the police. (We were wrong about this!)

Before deciding to go forward we needed to determine whether the project could be made profitable. One must be certain that there were no snags in the opportunity, such as unreasonable terms or legal problems. And one needed to know what the police really wanted. A simple museum showing its collection of memorabilia would not be financially viable. Would they go for something more exciting?

To win the business we needed to gain credibility by choosing the best team possible. These people had to be invited and to commit to come with us before our rivals approached them. This was urgent, but so was putting together an outline of what place they would have in the enterprise, what it would mean for them, and what the museum and related development would be like.

At this point we needed to express our interest and to ask questions but we would not decide to pitch for the job until we had done the homework that I describe in the first three chapters of this book. Subsequent chapters describe the work we did later and the project we planned to achieve. Chapters 5, 6, and 21-23 summarise the complicated property development that we had to achieve in order to go ahead with the museum. We worked on this in parallel with the museum planning. At the end of the book there is an account of why this property development and museum did not happen.

Throughout this book I shall use the word "Police" as a simple way of signifying the source of the views or requirements of the two Police Forces, (sometimes called Police Services) as conveyed to us through London Police Education Ltd. We always received a co-ordinated police view whatever differences there may have been within the Police Forces, except at the end when the project was being stopped.

Starting points

One of my first thoughts on reading the advert was that a museum of police memorabilia, uniforms, truncheons, and so forth would not attract enough visitors to cover its operating costs. The police wanted to attract people from a very wide circle, not just those interested in policing, and a museum of policemen's equipment would not do this. The tourism professionals who would create and manage the museum know that visitor attractions that attract lots of visitors have to enable people to interact with their content. And they have to be managed with the customers' interests and not the conservation of the objects uppermost.

The media carries police stories every day and so I thought that we could produce a mixture of human interest and technical know-how, which would be a winner. It would be like a mixture of The Sun and New Scientist. As most of our material would come from policing incidents we soon began to talk about it as a 'museum of incidents'. We would have to make this kind of museum interactive, to involve the media, to maintain topicality and to avoid confrontation with anti-police activists.

When we told the police that we were interested in the project we were sent more information on their intentions and were invited to view the former Bow Street Police Station. This was a Crown-owned building under the control of Philip Fletcher who, in those days, was the "Receiver for the Metropolitan Police District". He was legally a 'corporation sole', which is in effect a one-man quango controlling all the property and other assets of the Metropolitan Police Force. The role was abolished in 2000 and the assets that were his responsibility were passed to the newly created Metropolitan Police Authority. (It is a local authority which provides the Metropolitan Police with its resources and with guidance, but responsibility for all police actions lies with the Commissioner.)

At the empty building I met a retired Chief Superintendent, Alan Moss, whom the Police had appointed to look after the project. Alan was the Company Secretary and consultant to London Police Education Ltd. I never asked him directly, but I think he had conceived the project in the first place and now needed a midwife to deliver it. He is a very pleasant, shrewd, competent and energetic person to work with and he has a great knowledge of police history and practice. Whilst he was in some ways a member of our team he was careful never to "go native". On occasion he showed great loyalty to the Metropolitan Police.

Alan helped me to understand what the police wanted and filled in some of the background. He readily agreed that it would not be a traditional museum of objects in glass cases and he spoke about the problems of community policing which were of concern to the Police. My impression was that differences in culture were not a subject that the police would want to talk about in public, for this could aggravate tensions. In Chapter 7 this is explained further.

The building is listed as being of architectural or historic significance, Grade 2. The listing was obviously needed to protect the four-storey front facing the Royal Opera House, which is very impressive, but the interior consisted of small high rooms devoid of any character and divided from the original space to suit changing needs for police offices. The only large rooms were the basement cloakroom and the canteen on the first floor. There would need to be a clearout of interior walls, although those with fireplaces in them might need to stay so that the building did not lose structural strength.

The rear wall of the building is built in the dull yellow stock brick, which is so widely used all over central London. Punctuated by black down-pipes it towers grimly over a rear service yard under which there were storerooms and toilets. On two sides of the service yard there were ranges of police cells. Each cell was about six feet wide and twice that long and windows were set into the high ceilings. They each had their original heavy doors, a bench to sleep on and a toilet bowl. The fourth side of the yard was the custody building for the Magistrates Courts next door.

Usually a prison van was parked by the door to the service yard, having entered from Bow Street through an archway.

The back of the building faces a five-storey block of deck access flats built about a century ago. On the side opposite the Magistrates Courts is a building used as a telephone exchange with offices rented by The Design Council on its upper floors. Bow Street is not the busiest street in Covent Garden for pedestrians but it is heavily used.

The Police had previously submitted the project to the Millennium Commission for funding from the lottery but the details had not been developed enough to succeed against strong competition for the limited money available The design consultants who had worked on this scheme had proposed pulling down the back wall between the former Police Station and the service yard and then building an extension to increase the size of the museum. Because of my previous experience with listed building problems I was surprised by this proposal and checked it out with English Heritage who said that it was not acceptable. If we wanted more floor space they would accept a free-standing building in the service yard provided that the integrity of the existing building was maintained and that the older cell block was retained.

A collection of memorabilia, press cuttings, uniforms, personal equipment, pictures and other records belonging to the Metropolitan Police was housed in a warehouse in Charlton. It was not open to the public. If we were selected we would be invited to pick what we wanted for the new museum, on permanent loan. When I later visited this collection I felt that it was heavily orientated towards press cuttings, other written material, pictures and uniforms. It was light on the things normally found in museums. One would find it interesting to browse there with just a few people around, which was probably what happened when the collection was located in an upper room at Bow Street Police Station. A stream of visitors would not have been able to see much Nor would anyone be amused or impressed.

The Police wanted a big say in the content of the museum but they accepted that as they were not taking any commercial risks the final decisions would be ours. Provided they approved of the content they would endorse the museum and help with it's marketing - particularly to London schools. It would save them some of the costs of their schools liaison programmes. I remember £150,000 per year as the savings figure.

There would need to be some museum artefacts of course, and I soon realised that we did not have nearly enough space in Central London to house and display all of the objects available to us. No doubt more objects would be offered us as we went on. I also felt that traditional methods of display were rather limiting. This is a familiar problem for museums generally.

Our proposed solution was to use modern information technology to record and present (via CD/DVD or Internet download) the material we could not include in the visitor attraction. We called the totality of this material the Virtual Museum. There is more about it in Chapter 20.

The Consortium and its advisers

My own firm is a leisure and tourism consultancy which has no competence in building work, so I asked Tom Tinner, the regional director of the construction company John Mowlem and Company Plc. if his firm would join us in our tender and put up some initial capital. It agreed to do so. The firm worked on difficult projects in London and soon I discovered that it was one of the Metropolitan Police's favourite contractors. I also approached Heritage Projects, a division of Continuum, which is the leading operator of history-based visitor attractions in Britain, and it agreed to run the museum. Northcroft were tasked to be project managers and help with costings. Ernst and Young were pencilled in as financial advisers. Metropolis AV+FX would help us with the interactive elements of the museum.

A short while earlier I had met Sniez Torbarina at a seminar and she had shown me pictures of some of the architecture of Jestico and Whiles for whom she worked on building interiors. Although I know scores of other architects, I thought that this firm's experience of achieving award winning additions to listed buildings, often for the Government, might be useful, especially as I favoured the use of glass and steel for adding to the building rather than attempts to replicate the original materials and style. A meeting with their younger director, Tony Ingram, led to his keen and able leadership of the architectural work we needed, with James Tatham as the project architect.

By this time Will Baker was starting to back me up. He had just started his business as a development consultant after working as a consulting engineer with Acer. I did not want the project to collapse if anything happened to me and felt that my deteriorating eyesight might become a problem. Equally I needed someone wholly trustworthy with whom to talk over problems, and who could look after some matters for me. The formalisation of our relationship did not happen until our Company was set up in 1999.

The development

The only possible way for us to pay for the museum was to let part of the property to commercial tenants. At first we thought of studio-offices for the media and businesses supplying the police, plus shops and a large restaurant. These would benefit the museum. Our idea was that the commercial rents would provide an income stream which could be sold to an institution in return for the capital needed for the conversion and fit-out works. Thereafter the museum should pay its own way from the entry charges so that it could not fall into arrears and have to close. It was always our view that it had to earn enough to pay its own operating costs.

The business challenge was to obtain sufficient space and money for the museum to operate profitably, and enough lettable space at normal rents to generate a return on the capital invested in the whole project. That was the basis upon which the whole deal was put together. Later on we found that only offices were going to generate enough rental income and brought in a commercial developer, Salmon Harvester, to look after this side of things.

Starting on the museum design

There is a strong resemblance between making a visitor attraction and making a film. The creative process is similar and both need more than a script and content. To achieve commercial success they must both contain human interest, excellent production and presentation, and appealing stories. A film needs attractive stars. A visitor attraction needs to have tangibility and audience participation - otherwise it might as well be a film, book or newspaper! The title is important and I shall explain in Chapter 13 that as we were not creating a museum as the English know it we decided to call our show "The Beat".

David Lang from Heritage Projects and some other friends from the museum design sector were suggesting that I needed to write the story line, equivalent to a film script, before we began to consider how to make the visitor attraction. It could then be designed to make the most of this story line. Whilst I know a few museums where this approach has worked well, I did not think it would help us at all in this case. My reasons underlie our whole approach to the work on the project.

There was no single story available. The Police are engaged in thousands of different activities every day. Any evolution of their practices over the years might come from changes in the law and of societal attitudes, which were outside of our remit. Or it might come from technical advances such as the invention of the motorcar and radio. The story of the progressive adoption of new technology would probably revolve around politics and money availability rather than invention. This would be hard to present and of limited interest. The evolution of police practices to meet social changes over the decades would be more interesting, but only to people who knew about those changes. The ten-year-old who has not yet learnt how our present society functions would find it all very dull and incomprehensible.

A history book about police in London already existed in The Encyclopaedia of Scotland Yard, and Alan Moss gave me a copy. Other books provide a succession of stories of the more notable cases and incidents. A story line of this nature might possibly interest the well educated but would have "street cred" only if it was excessively over-dramatised - like the presentations at the London Dungeon. We had been specifically asked by the Police not to do anything like the London Dungeon.

These are arguable theoretical objections to writing a story line. The clincher was that in practice someone who well understands what interests the public would have to acquire a clear understanding of the facts, the cultural background within and without these two Police Forces, and their sensitivities, in order to set down an acceptable story line. That would be an enormous task. And what if the result was unsatisfactory? Who would then be to blame for the commercial failure? My conclusion was that because Will and I were taking the commercial risk no-body other than one of us could undertake this task. Neither of us had the time or inclination.

So we looked for another way forward. This was to divide the potential subject matter into *modules*, which we later came to call *scenarios* and finally *features*, and would ask different teams to do the research and creative work necessary to make the most of each one. We would ourselves need to know only enough detail to be able to select the features and manage the process. The number of features would exceed the space available so that we could replace those that seemed to be less interesting to customers.

This approach had the practical advantage that we could arrange the features within the museum in any way we liked, which helped in a building with a difficult layout for a museum. We need not decide the arrangement until after the conversion had been carried out - which very much simplified the internal design challenge. I liked it also because we could use different design teams for different features, according to their particular skills.

Of course there are disadvantages to this approach. We might lose design coherence, but that could be overcome by introducing a graphic-design co-ordinator and a good project manager to bring everything together. We would find it more difficult to explain what the outcome would be in advance of completing the design process. This was not going to help London Police Education so we had to work at explaining ourselves as we went along.

Meanwhile there were other important matters to consider.

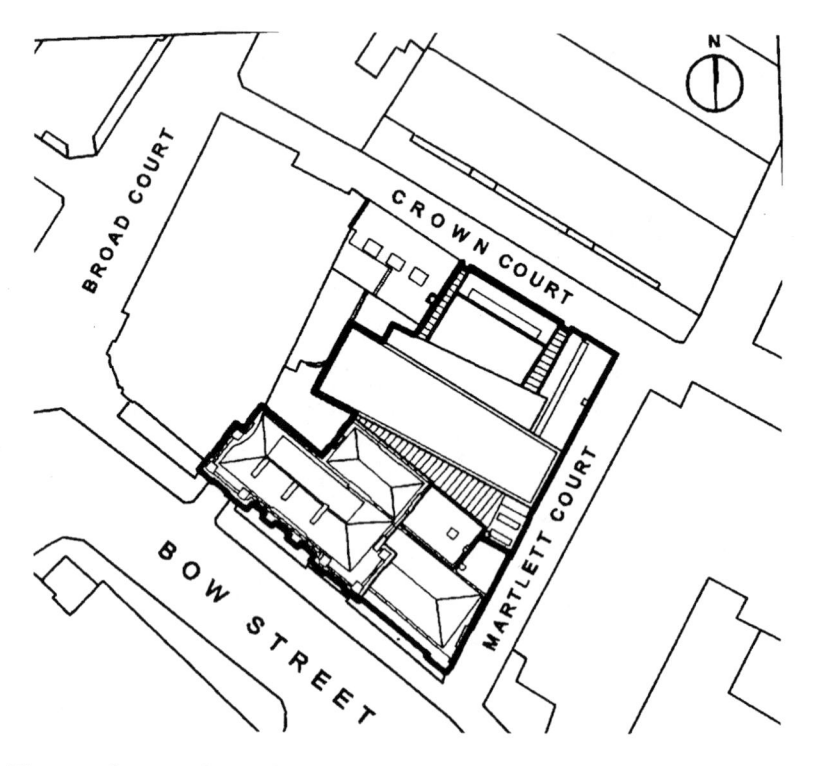

The site showing the outline of our proposed new blocks superimposed

2
Demand and supply

The London Police wanted us to start a business that would be new. They were not taking any of the commercial risk and did not know how great it was. I needed to be sure that this would be a good business before going on. Many people start businesses because they expect to enjoy running them and they too often omit to research whether there are enough people who might want their product or service for it to make a profit, or whether competitors will be able to damage them. Such businesses usually fail.

Wiser folk start businesses because the have seen a gap in the market that they are keen to fill. We needed to know whether there was, such a gap so we looked at the supply of police museums and competitive visitor attractions.

The Police had already commissioned market research to find out whether there would be a demand for the museum. The results were given to us and they confirmed that a well chosen sample of Londoners wanted a museum of the type we were proposing, although few of those interviewed said they would make a visit! The survey did not reveal anything useful about the quality and quantity of any demand, or tell us how much visitors would be prepared to pay to enter. As a businessman I thought it best to ignore the research but could see that the study had been useful in moving the study on.

London's private police museums

There was and is no museum of policing open to the public in London, although most other big cities have them. The Police have private museums within the headquarters of each force, at Hendon Police College, at the centres where they train their dogs and their horses. The river police have their own private museum at Wapping. The Metropolitan Police keeps a museum collection in a warehouse at Charlton.

The most notorious of these museums is in Scotland Yard. It is commonly called the Black Museum although its official name is the Crime Museum, and it contains things that have been used by criminals, many of which would have been presented to the jury in court. The museum is used for training police officers and entertaining VIP's.

In the hope of increasing understanding of what we were about and picking up some ideas I took nineteen of my team to see it. We were shown around by the curator John Ross, who provided an excellent commentary on the exhibits. He started by pointing to some knives used by murderers and saying that they had never been cleaned of their victim's blood. Most of us found the visit quite traumatic and agreed that it was too shocking for the public to see more than the replicas of small parts.

The most astute comment on it came to me afterwards from one of our consultants, John Stevenson, who wrote as follows: -

"It struck me, and possibly others, that the Black Museum didn't really have its own message. In fact it needn't have been anything to do with the police, except that the artefacts were all gained through policing. They could with a bit of imagination, have been gained through taking a macabre cross-section through a community. Moreover, having the hanging nooses on display with everything else gave one of the few messages from the law's side, even though there's nothing to say that only the law can hang people. I felt there were several types of exhibit with ambivalent messages, for example both criminals and the police use guns."

The City of London Police's private museum was good but much more traditional – glass cases, badges, uniforms *et al.*

Other attractions with a police theme

The Police did not want the proposed museum to be like the London Dungeon even though this is very successful in attracting visitors and hence would be our competitor. It is a macabre show about crime and punishment through the centuries, which is well managed, but totally alien to the serious mind of the modern policeman.

Will Baker went to see the two Sherlock Holmes visitor attractions in the Baker Street area. It led him to surmise that there was a possibility of devoting part of our museum to fictional police incidents, but he did not see these places as serious competition.

A researcher and I visited the public police museum in Manchester and found it very interesting, but visitor numbers were quite low. It contained some objects that came from London and would be better shown on their home ground.

Far more successful in attracting visitors is the "Galleries of Justice" in Nottingham. This is a good exhibition covering some of the same ground as we would, but survives on a heavy subsidy that is provided in order to meet some social objectives among young offenders. It is the kind of competitive enterprise that would be beneficial in building interest in the subject, to mutual advantage.

The competition

To be safe in our venture we had to ensure that no new rival police museum would start up during the fifteen years we would be trading and so we required the London Police Forces to agree that they would not endorse or support a rival. The *quid pro quo* for this exclusivity would be that our information had to be correct and acceptable to them, and it rather ruled out much fictional content except on the shelves in the shop.

We also had to review other types of competition. Visitor numbers in the busiest attractions in London in 1997, are set out in the table on the next page. These were collected and published by the English Tourism Council. They were provided by operators who determine how they are assembled, there being some discretion in this. Some of the attractions are free and entry charges at the others vary randomly.

In the immediate area of Bow Street this would come from the Theatre Museum, which is a bit specialist, and from the London Transport Museum which has much larger premises than we could obtain, full of big vehicles. Our view was that by being nearby we would all gain more visitors..

Many of the best attractions to visit in London are not centrally located. These include the Imperial War Museum at Dulwich, the Museum of Childhood at Bethnal Green, the Cutty Sark and National Maritime Museum at Greenwich, Kew Gardens, The Thames Barrier, Whitechapel Art Gallery, and Syon Park. It follows that our central location would give us an edge over these places. On the other hand the large number of interesting museum collections open to the public in many different places do not attract a high numbers of people, so these are not what we wanted to emulate.

Many visitors to attractions are more interested if there is something to do and they are not just looking. Nowadays all the better museums involve interactivity. There are various kinds of interactivity and I quickly recruited to our team people with knowledge of the tool kits for these. London is lagging behind in providing interactive experiences, perhaps because its attractions are longer established. There are a few good ones but we thought that being up-to –date and innovative would help us steal a march on rival.

The tasks of attracting visitors

To draw significant numbers of visitors we thought that we should harness the interest in police incidents which one can see in the daily flow of stories in the media, as well as the interest of some people in the technology of policing, such as forensics, communication systems and rescue equipment.

	'000
Museum of London	293
London Transport Museum	225
Theatre Museum	150
Tower Bridge	425
Museum of Childhood	75
National Army Museum	128
Courthauld Gallery	81
Design Museum	134
Horniman Museum	222
RAF Museum	140
Serpentine Gallery	203
Kensington Palace	60
Queens Gallery	77
Globe Theatre	188
Imperial War Museum	518
Royal Academy exhibitions	140
Wallace Collection	190
Whitechapel Art Gallery	116
Old Bailey	85
Albert Memorial	81
Madame Tussaudss	2,700
British Museum	6,200
National Gallery	4,800
National Portrait Gallery	883
Natural History Museum	1,700
Tate Gallery	1,700
Tower of London	2,600
V & A	1,000

We planned to gain the fame that would make The Beat a "must see" place, like Madame Tussauds or The Tower of London. A good starting point for this was to attract children who needed to learn about the police, serving police officers from this country and abroad, and everyone else working in law and order professions. We could also provide an expert service to journalists and press photographers. All we had to do was to ensure that our product was of a high standard so that it would be universally praised. No small challenge!

DEMAND AND SUPPLY

On reviewing the overall situation of demand and supply there seemed to be plenty of demand for a niche product in this location, and no likelihood of that demand being met by anyone else if we proceeded in the right way – and achieved a strong presence on the Web, and in the public mind.

The main entrance for visitors - the first design

4

We needed some numbers

One of the questions that we were asked time and again for years was :- "How many people are you expecting to attract? "

The question was asked by the Police, by our architects and service engineers who had to make calculations, by the museum designers and by the media. The questioners all assumed that this could be forecast. I did not think it could. The classic method used by leisure developers to forecast demand is to look at similar products in other places and assume that with competent management and marketing the number of visitors will be about the same, or a little larger or smaller. This is fine if you are rolling out near identical Casinos or Sealife Centres, but not so good if your product is unique.

Visitor attractions are like films. People go to see them if they become famous, regardless of the number of other films available. Lesser films may attract people with a particular interest in their content or style, but they are more vulnerable to good competition. For a film maker as well as a leisure developer, estimating demand is not a simple process because logically one cannot measure demand for a product that is not yet available, and because visitor experiences compete with one another even when they are very different in kind. People say to one another "What shall we do?" Few of them say, "What museum shall we go to?"

The Police and the respondents to their survey could not tell us what exactly they wanted because they did not know what we could provide. Nor was anyone sure how they themselves would feel and react when they learnt things about the police.

It is possible to find an answer to such a question where there are similar products in similar locations with which one can make comparison. But our product would be new, and my experience is that it is not possible to make a forecast of sales for a new product.

So when I was asked this question I always replied that it would be between two and five hundred thousand visitors a year and I could not be more precise. If pressed, I explained that the total annual number of visitors would depend upon the publicity we attracted, the current competition, the extent to which we received repeat visits, our marketing skills, and the quality, educational value, tastefulness and attractiveness of the content. The attitude to the museum of police officers whether they are serving or retired would also be important.

Until the museum/attraction was up and running it was as difficult to forecast "box office" takings as it would be for a film in the making. As with a film, relatively few people come to a visitor attraction twice. Its reputation based on quality and popular appeal is what determines the numbers. My cautious approach to this was amply justified a couple of years later when consultant forecasts of the number of visitors to The Millennium Dome turned out to be wildly optimistic. Several other projects had this problem. Conversely, there are places such as Yorvik where the opposite occurred. It was always in our minds that we might have to keep the total number of visitors down to the building capacity by means such as requiring advanced booking – as did The London Eye in its early years.

And no, there was no secret number that was more precise. Of course I could have invented a number to suit the occasion, as some attraction developers do. But I felt that it was better not to reply either by giving the number that the questioner wanted to hear, or the number which would attract most financial and political support. To do either would have been dishonest and was not really necessary.

There was one exception. We had to show our confidence in our ability to draw people when we were at the selection interview and so on that day we tentatively adopted the number suggested by the Police's museum consultant which was 375,000 visitors a year - even though I had my doubts. There are only about two score visitor attractions in Britain that attract more than 300,000 visitors a year. Even our subject matter and location would be unlikely to lift us far above this figure. In London, competition is said to be fierce and there are surprisingly few attractions that are in our expected bracket. A few are much bigger, but most are much smaller. The Museum of London, Tower Bridge and London Transport Museum are comparable with the lower end of our bracket.

How did we decide our upper and lower forecasts? The upper number of 500,000 is a little above the comfortable capacity of the space available. The different types of visitor for which this is the aggregate are described in Chapter 8. We found out when the conversion plans were drawn up that the building could not take enough people at peak times to go much above 400,000 visitors a year, and so the number could only be reached if we were very successful in obtaining evening functions and in bringing school parties there on quiet winter days.

Our minimum number, 200,000 was a little below the number required to break even financially. The business would have to close or be given away to a charity if our numbers were below that. So this figure would not be too high!

Later on, the architects and the heating engineers needed to know the peak numbers at any one time rather than the annual numbers that there would be in the building. We needed fire escapes that would never be congested. We needed to decide how to heat the place on a cold February morning when there was hardly anyone there. We could foresee great difficulty in keeping it cool on a peak day during a summer heat wave, especially bearing in mind that the air conditioning intakes would be drawing from the very hot adjoining streets.

Should we limit admissions on such days? I thought that it might be more economic to save on cooling plant costs and limit numbers when it got too hot. This is easier said than done because the estimation of heat build-up is based on many assumptions and engineers are trained to be cautious. I reckon that our reasoning with our consultants would have to be based upon the political concept called sustainability and not on finance.

Entry charges

We decided that our entry charges would be no more and no less than "what the market will bear" for the size and quality of attraction we would create. Lower charges for anyone whom the Police specifically wanted to subsidise such as school children would be paid for out of London Police Education's share of the profit - which was actually a royalty we would pay them.

Our view was that the charge that the market would bear would be about £6.50 per adult in 1998 values, but later this was revised upwards. Children, senior citizens and groups would pay the usual proportion of this. Using this figure, the initial business plan showed that the break-even figure for operations was about 230,000 visitors a year. When alternative visitor numbers or charges were used as a multiplier we had a range of figures to show in the sensitivity tests required for the business plan!

Business planning

The Police made it quite clear that they needed to be satisfied with our business plan before they could select us. My first task in preparing this plan was to decide the business structure. Following a widespread practice in the museum sector I assumed that the museum operating company would rent the building and create the museum inside it. This Company would then collect the admission charges, retail sales proceeds and lesser revenues. It would staff and run the museum, refurbishing it from time to time. After looking at the figures I did not think that the ten-year tenure proposed by the Police was long enough for us to proceed successfully and therefore suggested fifteen years for this, which was accepted.

Preparing the business plan for this operating company followed well-established practices in the leisure industry and was quite easy for me to do as I had comparable figures at hand. I checked these with Heritage Projects, which as an operating firm had detailed experience of costs.

The main operating cost for a visitor attraction is staffing. It is horrific the way in which this has gone up in recent years due to staff overheads such as training, pensions, maternity leave and similar rights, not to mention inflation in central London house prices. So we worked out that we could not afford staff to run features or answer questions. The place would have to run itself with staff to deal only with marketing, school parties, security, cleaning, and other maintenance problems. The shop income would cover its own staffing. There might be volunteer help available to visitors.

Without a detailed design for the museum we could not work out the cost of fitting it out. But one must design to a budget. This "catch 22" was most awkward. I decided to pull a figure off the wall. It was £3M, plus what we could raise by sponsorship or the leasing of exhibits and equipment. This figure is low by modern exhibition standards. The reason for plumping for a low figure was partly to do with financing and partly because the subject matter did not require high cost exhibits. The designers would want to spend more, but it wasn't necessary.

We later decided to opt for exhibits that might have a short-term life in this location and replace them frequently rather than try to build in robustness to the degree that some discovery-centres do. I have no qualms about this because over-engineered interactives often get in the way of understanding the basics of how they work. Simple exhibits made of easily available materials are better at stimulating kids to try to make their own. The simplest things can be effective in communication. Extremely robust exhibits may be long lasting and classy but I doubt that they are cost-effective. They are better used where capital for fitting out comes from grants and is seen as "free", and non-replaceable.

We allowed £1 per visitor per annum for upgrading and refurbishments of the exhibits. This is equivalent to a ten year life following which there would be comprehensive refurbishment. In practice, three-yearly programmes of partial refurbishment would make more sense. We expected to pay for some upgrading by means of sponsorship. Whether we could get much sponsorship would be uncertain until the museum was up and running and we could show it to possible sponsors, together with the visitor number records.

At first we thought that we would have the museum space rent free but during negotiations with Salmon Harvester we agreed to pay a rent This was about £6 per square foot per annum which s far below market rents in this part of London. Without this rent, guaranteed by the Metropolitan Police Authority, financing would not have been possible. In Chapter 24 I shall explain why it became a problem later.

We had trouble establishing the rateable value for the museum. Museums are such strange creatures in this respect that the professional valuer will not provide advice. Our guess for this was not very well informed!

The business plan for the operations was revised several times and on each occasion was shown to the Police. It was used to explain why it was not economic to run a smaller museum with fewer visitors than one having about 20,000 sq.ft. of gross internal space. Like nearly all financial estimates for visitor attractions it showed that if we fell below break-even visitor numbers we had dire problems, if we had many more visitors we would make a very attractive profit indeed.

At this stage I discussed with Heritage Projects the possibility of that company leasing the museum and running it for us. The reply was that they did not wish to take the risk. I thought that this was a reasonable view given that they would not be controlling the content and I explained to the Police that Heritage Projects would be managers rather than risk-bearing operators.

Development appraisal

We also told the Police that in order to generate the revenue needed to give the return required by the finance market for its capital investment our proposal was that a quite separate company would hold on lease and develop the property, letting out some space commercially and the rest to us. The Metropolitan Police Receiver had decided not to sell the freehold of the building but wanted us to take a lease by paying a premium and a nominal rent

The investment capital would be used to pay the conversion costs, the initial fit-out cost for the museum, and the lease premium.. The amount of finance required was estimated on the understanding, based on my experience, that we would not be able to obtain grant funding nor borrow very much of the cost of fitting out the museum.

It was unlikely that this capital could be raised at a profitable rate prior to the conversion and fit-out works being completed. Certainly this was not possible before we had even obtained planning consent. So we had to look at a two-stage process. Initially development capital would be provided (by Mowlem we proposed then). This capital would be replaced later by long term financing. A very simple business plan would be required at this second stage, but for the first stage we had to prepare what is known as a development appraisal.

Initially, all we had by way of figures was the lease purchase price pencilled in at about £2-2.5M on the guidance of the Police. As already mentioned I put in £3M for the fit-out of the museum. Our cost consultants, Northcroft, ran their computers over the architects' initial plans and indicated the total cost of alterations and additional construction. The usual provisions for finance costs, professional fees and tenancy marketing were added. The commercial uses of the building were going to be a large restaurant, small offices and shops. I shall explain later why these were changed to high quality offices alone and both the costs and rental income had to be recalculated.

Every time the plans were changed the figure was adjusted and Salmon Harvester (when they later joined us) used their usual quantity surveyor, The Wheeler Group, to provide much more detail. It turned out that the building was particularly expensive to alter effectively because of its layout and structure.

The quality of the original building is high. The interior could be changed. This gave us the opportunity to offer the development to the market as a trophy building in a central location where rents could be high. From this starting point we were committed to high quality in the building alteration works. But we could and did assume that the rents achievable would be comparably high and letting would be quick. On more than one occasion we obtained agents advice on the rents that could be obtained. At first this was from Davis Coffer Lyon, restaurant specialist and later from Farebrother, office specialist.

Risks and calculations

Given the subjectivity of many key numbers used in our successive business plans and development appraisals one might ask whether the commercial risks were acceptable. The reply would have been as that the risks were moderate provided that we removed all possible uncertainties before we committed. So every risk was examined, and changes were made so that they were minimised. I have not seen any project better thought out by the developers than was this one.

In this book I am not going to say any more about the business planning, but from time to time we had to update our original numbers to make sure that the project was still profitable. Extra costs did appear. For instance we had to pay for archaeological surveys, which showed that the houses that preceded the Police Station were built in fields belonging to a convent These fields lay, during the Middle Ages, over the remains of the Saxon city that was called Lundwich. Saxon remains were found on a nearby site.

There were unforeseen costs too for security measures required by the Magistrates' Courts next door, for fire escape arrangements, letting fees, and air-conditioning because it was very difficult to find a position for a large fresh air intake that did not wake the neighbours or alter the outside of the listed building. The figures were such that during one period when commercial rents were falling but construction costs were rising it was not a commercially attractive proposition. This is just the swing of the development pendulum which can damage property profits.

The architect's sketch of the museum interior – the first scheme

4
The selection

After five months of waiting, the police were getting their act together by June 1998. My colleagues, and executives from our partners, Mowlem, were filling in an elaborate questionnaire. The architects were working with me on our plans for erecting a new building in the service yard at the rear of the police station. This would double the floor space available and give us easily used open floors at five levels, linked by bridges to the old building. We had to produce sketches of this so that the police could see what we intended. Our cost consultants, Northcroft, needed the sketches so that they could tell us what the works would cost, a key figure before we could decide whether it would be profitable to go ahead.

All this work was being done without any payments, so the firms doing it took a keen interest in our views on whether we would get the contract. They could see we had a first class team and that I had so much planning experience that permission would not be refused. They did not know where and when I was going to raise the finance. They trusted the Police.

More thinking was necessary to work out the best way to structure the consortium arrangements and contracts. The development work had to be separated from the fit-out of the museum and this from the subsequent operations.

We decided not to seek the VAT advantage of making the museum a charity as this would have limited our control of the content and operation and the risks for everyone would have been greater. It was enough that it would probably become charitable after our ten-year tenancy (the contract later extended this to fifteen years).

The business structure had to be explained in some detail to the Police who were unfamiliar with the way developers work to minimise risk. I wanted the Police to have a financial stake in the museum operating company to ensure that they did not impose their ideas to our commercial detriment. Although some local authorities do this, the Police said they could not do so because of the risks of failure rebounding on the public purse and their reputation. They accepted that this meant they did not have the final say in what we put in to the museum.

Having put our ideas together in textual form and passed them forward, we had to present some sound proposals for the museum that were obviously more exciting, relevant and sensitive to Police concerns than those of our competitors. Whilst I did not then know whom we were competing against I knew enough about the business to assume that they did not include any of the large firms like Madame Tussaudss, Merlin or Disney. We had Heritage Projects with us. However, there were other people such as developers who might have hired the firm that produced sketch designs for the previous Millennium bid by the Police - or similar designers. We needed to do better.

I looked for a way to present visually and in a few hundred words the embryonic concept that was in our minds. Truly, we had only a vague idea of what the police stories might be and of the content of the Police museum collections from which they said we could draw.

A Manchester leisure design consultancy called Eigg prepared some drawings to show the Police what it would look like inside. (Below)

Tender by *THORBURNS and MOWLEM*

Draft text for tourist promotion leaflet:-

BLUE LAMPS

Put yourself in the shoes (or the uniform) of a London Policeman or Policewoman and decide what you are going to do when you -

- meet a rowdy crowd in the street,
- arrive at the scene of a tragedy,
- are running a road control check,
- have to act on receiving a 999 call,
- need to re-route an ambulance up by a demonstration,
- tell TV what is happening,
- take fingerprints and mugshots,
- prosecute in court
- are set a tricky forensic puzzle
- need to choose a dog for a task,
- see trouble from a police control van,
- are called to a suspect package
- are learning to be a bodyguard

You can choose for your visit an on-screen personal copper to help you cope with these situations or just to answer queries. You can start your "visit" on the Internet before you come, and finish it after you have gone home. Take home a recording of your visit.

Blue Lamps is in Bow Street, Covent Garden, the home of the first police force in Britain. It has many more things to do and see, all based on genuine police incidents, and supported by the unique heritage collection of London police uniforms and equipment. Dress up in old-style uniforms. Visit the old cells. Hear true stories of police adventures in the past - and view the latest equipment, and IT systems.

Meet police celebrities and TV stars.

Visit "The Peelers" restaurant, the "Runners" winebar, or "The Dockgreen" tearoom. Select from our unique souvenirs.

Blue Lamps is in the old Bow Street Police Station - opposite the Royal Opera House.

Open 10.00 - 8.00 every day. Covent Garden tube station.
Admission: adult £5.90. Children £4.40. Group rates. Telephone 0171 430 1911

We had written down a description of the museum as we saw it at that time, and called it "Blue Lamps". To convey its nature as simply as possible I wrote a tourist leaflet on one side of paper, which is reproduced opposite.

Our competitors

In July we received a letter from Alan Moss, Company Secretary of London Police Education Ltd., saying that we were one of four shortlisted firms. Several years later I found out that our three rivals were Vardon Attractions, AYH and Adventure Projects. We were separately invited to clarification meetings with him and officials at which the discussion included a string of questions arising from the information we had provided. I did not feel that this was difficult.

Vardon Attractions saw themselves as 'edutainment' specialists in a unique London market and they proposed live entertainment and theatre based within the museum. They envisaged finding other firms to unlock the property values. At the time their relevant Division was being hived off from their parent company. They asked for a very substantial return on minimal capital and their financial strength and commitment was not clear.

A former client told me at the time that David Collison, a man with a background in theatre productions, was one of our competitors. I did not know him already or contact him, but went to see his visitor attraction in Hastings. It was entertaining and well done but less seriously educational than that which the police had in mind. I wondered how they would get on. (It turned out that his creative designs had impressed the Board of London Police Education)

Adventure Projects, David Collison's firm, had teamed up with a small property developer. They proposed some residential development and had worked out their financial structure but not the way of finding enough capital. They did not want to buy the building.

AYH were originally quantity surveyors and they had proposed for the site the commercial development of flats and a comparatively small museum partly in a new building. Jonathan Bryant, for whom I have a high regard, was the museum specialist in their team.

The day came in September 1998 when we were invited to sit around a large table in Scotland Yard and to present our scheme to the board members of London Police Education Ltd. These were Paul Manning, (MET Assistant Commissioner), Philip Fletcher, (The Receiver) Reginald Watts (a member of the Metropolitan Police Committee), and Tom Jackson (Chairman of City of London Police Committee). Perry Nove

THE SELECTION

(City of London Police Commissioner) was not available that day but was present when we were selected. Professional and union advisers were also there.

By way of introduction I summarised our proposal, drew attention to the main problems and proffered our solutions as set out below. I explained the drawings of the museum interior and what it would be like

Tony Ingram showed his architectural drawings and explained the building works proposed.

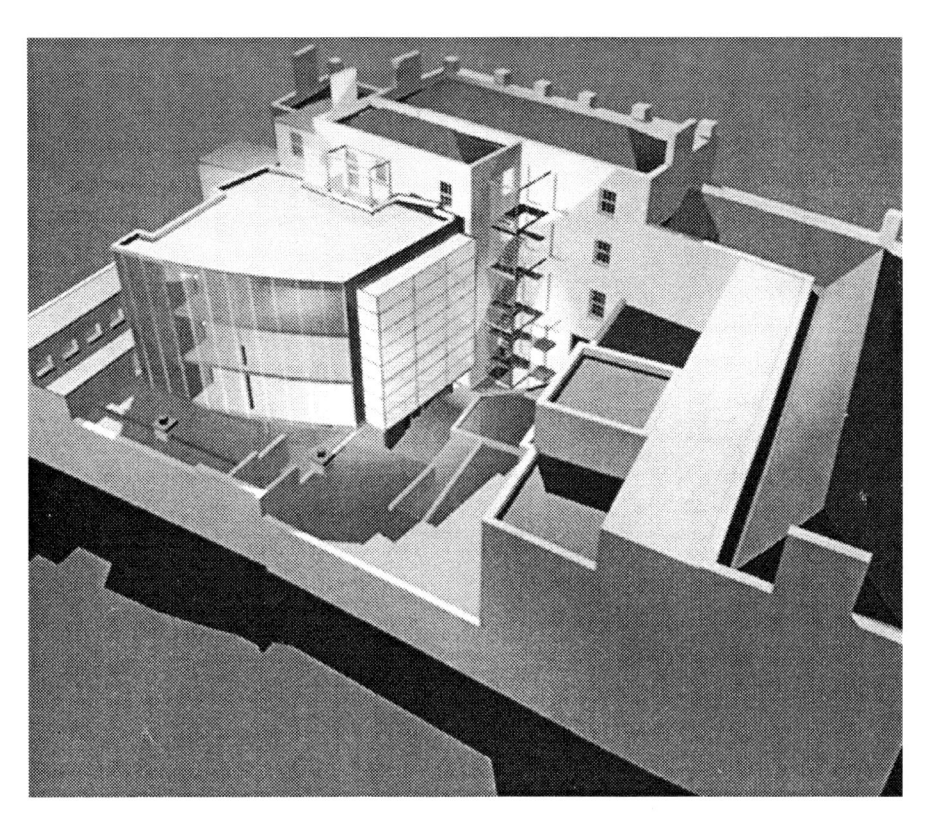

The first model of our proposals　　　　Jestico and Whiles, architects

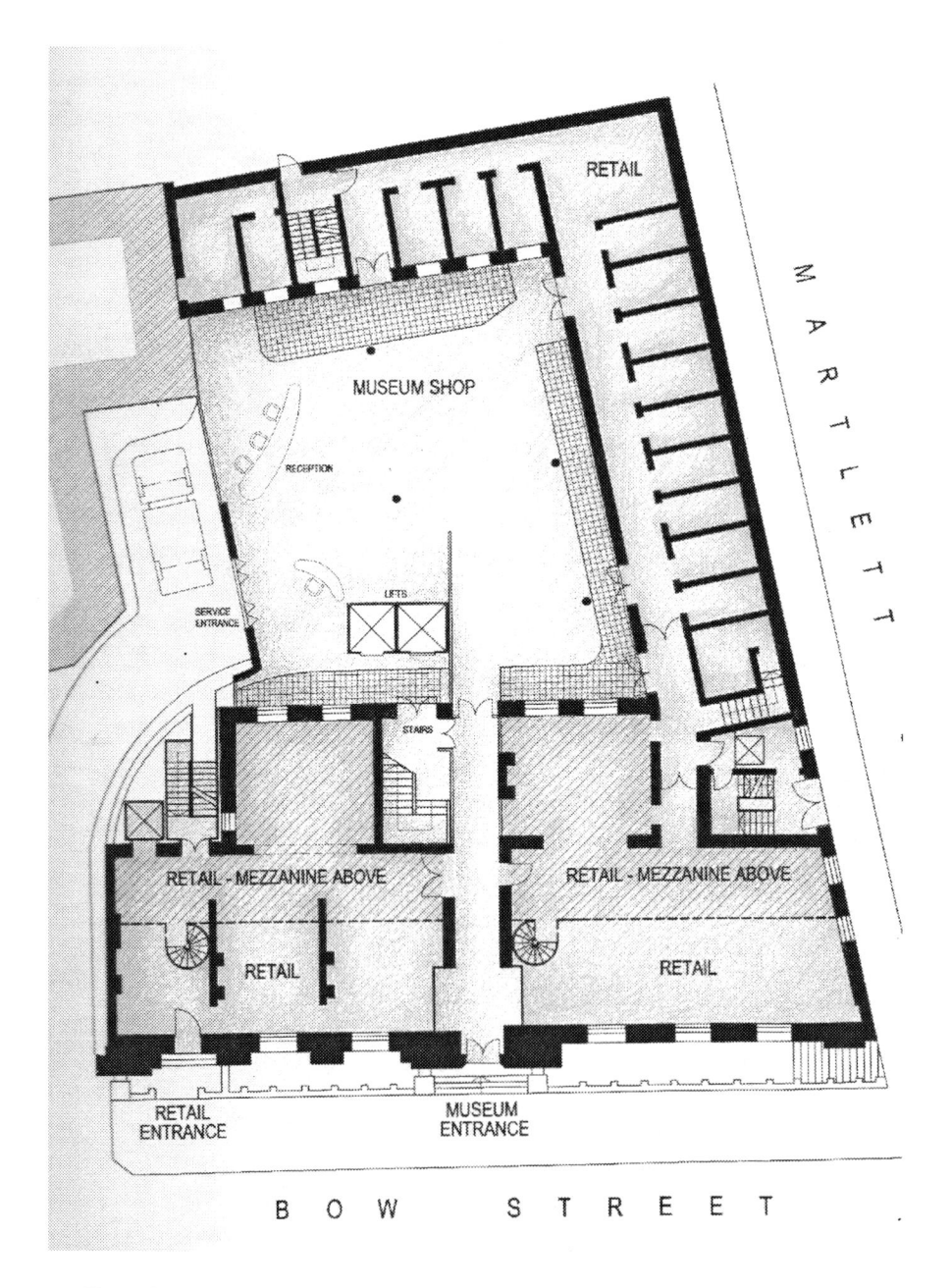

The plan of the ground floor as proposed in our submission

Assuming that the Board would be familiar with modern consultants jargon I presented our approach as the solutions to the problems we knew they would face. This is the note I used to brief them.

Tender by THORBURNS and MOWLEM

THE PROBLEMS and THE SOLUTIONS

No money available from Police	Sale and lease back of building
Need for reliable income to pay lease rent	Lease commercial areas to large firm
Insufficient money	Enhance property value by new build
	Increase commercially let area
	Simplify project negotiations
	Do not use developer
	Structure to minimise VAT
	Create sponsorship opportunities
Up-front cash needed	Construction company finance at first
Planning permission uncertain	Create scheme attractive to planners – the uses, impact, conservation
	Planner leading the team
Objections from English Heritage	Protect integrity of building
	Display heritage elements of building
	Heritage experienced Architects, plann
Entrances too small	Reopen former entrance
Not enough space	Build new building in yard
	Lower ceiling height in new build
	Galleries inside old building
	Remove some internal walls
High quality management scarcity	Select leading attraction operator

Ensuring co-operation by key players	Use joint venture company:
	    Thorburns
	    Mowlem
	    London Police Education
	    Heritage Projects
	    Lead tenant (Whitbread)
	Open books for all involved,

Need for Police control of museum	Police half-own operating company
Uncertainty, and costs of delay	Minimise third party approvals Do not rely on grant aid
Young people not interested in museums	Use name such as "BLUE LAMPS" Integrate exhibits with activities Liven with most advanced interactives Activate TV and Internet links
Human wariness of the Police	Make entrance very user friendly Avoid using "police" in the title Encourage police-associated visitors Theme policing more than the police Design for better understanding"
Commercial risk is high	Avoid relying on museum income , Link uses with Royal Opera House Use fast and flexible decision process Minimise contract writing' , . , . Building team used to Inner London
London Police Education needs income	Covenant part of operating surplus

THE SELECTION

Tom Tinner explained Mowlem's contribution enthusiastically and David Lang spoke of Heritage Projects successful attractions in York, Oxford, Canterbury and Tunbridge Wells. Will Baker enlarged on some key matters.

When our turn came to ask questions we requested promises that, as we went along, there would be no delays in responding to any matter we raised with the Police, and that the property was definitely available at market value. Given the nature of large organisations wherein not everyone may be singing the same tune, I thought that these two specific assurances were very important. They were put into contracts and honoured for several years but eventually were breached, as I had feared. The last two chapters of this book will explain.

Adventure Projects was interviewed several weeks after ourselves and after this London Police Education decided to ask this firm and ourselves for further information. So it was another six weeks before we heard that we had been selected. We celebrated, and set up a company which we called Bow Street Partners Ltd as the "special purpose vehicle" to implement the project.

There were two separate streams of work ahead. One was to plan, design and fit out the museum. The other was to obtain the money, design the alterations to the building, obtain planning consent, carry out the works and finally let the building sufficiently profitably to finance everything.

As explained in the next chapter, we selected a property developer, Salmon Harvester Ltd., as our partner firm to do the latter although I continued to be involved personally as future tenant, town planner, liaison officer and so forth. Much of my next two years were to be spent on these complex matters but they are not a story that needs to be told in detail. This work is summarised in Chapters 21-23. However, this book is primarily about the museum and that is the concern of Chapters 7-20.

Only when not busy on development matters could Will Baker and I turn to considering what the museum would contain. Our aim was to carry the Police with us in our thinking, and to provide a visitor attraction that would be easy and profitable for Heritage Projects to run. Our proposals had to fit into the building, and had to be financially realistic. Being selected to take the project forward did not mean that our ideas were sufficiently clear to provide a brief for a design team. They weren't for more than two years.

Blue Lamps: London Police Museum

Tender by **THORBURNS** *and* **MOWLEM**

KEY ELEMENTS OF OUR PROPOSAL FOR THE

LONDON POLICE MUSEUM

1. Set up joint venture company to develop the Museum and run it for ten years, with shareholdings held by the key firms involved,

2. Buy, alter and add to the building to maximise the space available, using Mowlem finance, *cost estimate £7.5M*

3. Sell and lease back the completed building for 125 years, *sale price estimate £10M*

4. To create value, let the lower half of the building for restaurants, winebar and related shopping, *rent estimate £600k*

5. Use the upper half of the building for the museum - featuring visitor participation in simulated police activities drawn from past incidents, and excellent media links, *net surplus income to be used for refurbishment and dividends to joint venture company,*

6. Operate the museum through a subsidiary company half owned by London Police Education Ltd., and run by the professional operators - Heritage Projects Ltd.

5
Raising the money

At our selection meeting we promised the Police that we would spend money we hadn't got, on a project we had not fully costed, to achieve a so-called museum, which the Police wanted - but either would not or could not pay for! Any figure for the museum budget was going to be an invention at this stage. I invented a budget of £3M. It might or might not be the right figure, but I had to be confident it was right in order to be convincing. Later we would come back to the detail of its assessment and division into different items. For now everybody was happy!

To understand why we could make such promises a little explanation is needed. There are thousands of organisations that have large amounts of money to sell every day, of which pension funds and the insurance companies with their daily inflow of premiums are typical example. They compete for the chance to provide finance to the best buyers, just like the farmers in a vegetable market. There is never any shortage of investment capital, but there can be a shortage of good places to put it, or, to put it another way, of good sound buyers. It is the unsound buyers or those who are unlucky enough to live in a high-risk country who complain of shortage of money.

We needed money for four purposes, and the purchase price of this would reflect the different type and degree of risk. Investors differ in the level and type of risks they will accept

At the start we had to carry out surveys, prepare plans and negotiate contracts. Whilst I was willing to risk £20-30,000 of my own money to do this I knew that we would need much more than this. Some of the professional firms were willing to speculate a little but others had to be paid at once. Mowlem our partner covered this. Businesses like Mowlem have to do considerable work to win a large contract and working with us was potentially cost-effective because otherwise they were going to have to compete for the job. Our joint total expenditure at the early stage was about £170,000, recoverable only when the contracts were all signed.

Next, we would need about £10-12M of high risk money to finance the acquisition and conversion of the property. The people who provide this kind of money are more interested in the competence of the executive team than in the nature of the project, but they take a close look at the development risks that have to be taken, especially delays.

Just as soon as the works are completed and the property is let to generate income this high risk money, which is inevitably expensive, will be wanted for another project. So low risk long-term money would be required to be invested in the property indefinitely. This money had to be in place, that is committed, before we could obtain any of the high-risk money which we needed first.

Additionally, a few more million pounds would be needed to design, fit-out and start up the museum. I knew that no one would lend me any money for this. Raising money for untried products is very difficult even when they are fully designed. I also knew that the design costs for a visitor attraction are never less than 25% of the total costs – or in this case at least £750,000. We did not have that money and therefore could not expect to borrow the rest of the cost of the museum. The money had to be obtained in a different way.

The possibilities were grants, sponsorship, lease finance of equipment, the equivalent of the "angels" who finance film making, or we could add it to the cost of carrying out the conversion works and thereby reduce the profit available from the development project as a whole when it is re-financed.

Right at the beginning of the project we decided not to try to finance it with grants. Like many consultants I had become disillusioned with the costs of preparing grant submissions and the poor return, if any, one can achieve. The Heritage Lottery Fund was no longer grant aiding new museums and there were few grants available in London.

Finance from sponsorship, investment by "angels", or leasing of equipment could not be quantified until we had worked out concepts and assembled the design and operating teams. Later it turned out that there was potential to add to the initial financing by sponsorship and leasing. This we intended to pursue in order to enlarge our budget. We never looked for "angels".

It was clear to me that our finance for the museum would have to come out of the development profit. To make the figures work out for the financier we had to enhance the profit by paying rent for the museum space from our entry fee income – which had not been our original intention. Had the museum failed the space could have been let to someone else, so this risk was not a problem.

When London Police Education selected us as preferred private sector partner we knew that we would have to lease the property from the Receiver for the Metropolitan Police District at market value. So we immediately entered into discussions with the property department of the Metropolitan Police Service to ascertain how much we should pay for a long lease. Market value depended partly upon the planning permission which could be obtained, bearing in mind that we were told by the planners that the building had no existing use rights for anything except a police station. No-one wanted it as a police station so it had no value other than what is known as "hope value".

The discussions were not confrontational as we were meeting a requirement and not haggling. We had received a fax in August 1998, before we were selected, which told us that the valuation of Bow Street police station at £2.2M was carried out on 20th March 1995 and the revised valuation of £3M was an in-house estimate of the subsequent increase in property values driven apparently by a rise in central London rents. We were also told that "there are some pressures on the Metropolitan Police budget which would tend to militate against a lower sum than an up-dated valuation being acceptable".

Not surprisingly, the Receiver for the Metropolitan Police wanted this figure updated and called in independent valuers, Gooch Webster. I was asked to show these valuers our business plan and went along to their offices to explain how the figures for operating surplus had been derived.

I was also asked to state our offer for the lease. In March 1999 our new Company, Bow Street Partners Ltd., made an offer of £2.0M. I meant to deduct from this the cost of works to relocate the cells used by the magistrates courts which were on offer to us (about £250k), but this got left out of the letter! The figure was accepted on May 19th 1999 and we were ready to go out and raise the money we needed.

In view of what happened later I should add that at the time I was told that the figure we offered had been cleared with the Home Office and the Treasury and was close to the independent valuation. It was not until 2003 that I saw this valuation and found that when it was made in February 1999 the valuers put a figure of £2.8M on the site conditional upon getting planning permission for housing and offices only, which was not practical given the planners requirement for a community use in the building. The scheme which the valuers thought most likely to get planning permission was for a restaurant and offices with residential to the rear within the existing building footprint. This was valued at £2.1M, but personally I think that there was no chance of getting permission for this. The planners were strongly against a restaurant and would have won on appeal. They would have continued to demand a community use. Moreover, English Heritage was insisting upon preservation of the cells and this would have reduced the value to £1,75M – which is exactly what I intended to offer prior to the mistake in my letter!

Diverging for a moment from the sequence of my story, my conclusion with the benefit of this knowledge is that my offer for the lease in March 1999 was generous. I am not surprised that it was quickly accepted. When they joined us, Salmon Harvester took the same view and wanted to negotiate it downwards! I asked the firm to hold back in order not to upset the Metropolitan Police. This matter of valuation was fundamental to the project and its demise, and I shall comment further in Chapters 24 and 25.

At the time, the way I looked at our situation was simple. In valuation theory the market value is the residue after all costs and profits have been taken into account. In this case the basis was hope value and the valuation depended entirely upon the view taken of what the planning authority would permit. In reality we were proposing to fund the whole scheme by converting this hope value into real value by obtaining a more beneficial planning consent than would be obtainable without the museum. Our ability to do this was unique not just because of our thorough knowledge of the planning system but because we could ourselves deliver the desired museum and thereby justify exceptions to policy.

Fundamentally I can best explain this by as a situation which required a balancing of interests and not a negotiation because there were too many different parties with conflicting interests to proceed in the normal way of a property deal. Obviously we would have to pay the market rate for money and ensure that we did not exceed budgets. There were a number of uncertainties such as: -

- What the market rate for money would be.
- Whether we would get the proposed planning permission.
- How much planning gain we would have to pay.
- What the museum design and fit out would actually cost.
- What income we would generate.
- The division of the floor space in the building between the museum and the commercial uses.

Our proposed plan for the property is described in Chapter 21. It seemed to be a fair balance between the interests of the property developer providing the money and skills, the asset owning arm of the Police, the Planning Authority, the public living nearby, the police museum interest and the operator. All might ask for more, and if things went badly the project might to be re-balanced. My role was that of honest broker in this and I was not intent upon maximising my interest as some of the other parties were. Alan Moss understood this and no doubt indicated the position to London Police Education.

By May 1998 we had a deal and had now to raise the money for the lease and for the development as set out in our development appraisal. Mowlem was no longer keen to put up enough money to carry out the works as they had become fully committed elsewhere. I had been introduced during a meeting on a different project to Neil Holmes, a former senior partner in Jones Lang, the large Chartered Surveying firm. It seemed to me that it might be better to ask him to help us than use a large firm such as the big Accountants. We retained him and he quickly obtained the interest of a merchant bank.

Our intention at that time was to retain Northcroft to manage the building work and retain agents for the marketing, using Bow Street Partners as the 'special purpose vehicle' vehicle which would hold the purse-strings. To put this together we would have needed to find a substantial sum as a commitment fee for the bank, at least £150,000 and I was unsure where we would find this.

However, a few months later a change of policy led to the bank withdrawing. So Neil went to about fourteen different developers he knew well to find out if they were interested in coming in with us. Five met us and entered into negotiations. Two of these, Salmon Harvester Ltd and Rugby Estates plc., offered almost identical terms, and based on the chemistry between us and their executives we chose Salmon Harvester and obtained the approval of the Metropolitan Police to bring them on board.

Salmon Harvester is jointly owned by NFU Mutual Insurance Company and Salmon Developments, which is a private development company with an excellent track record. Paul Stoodley was their development director and most of my dealings were with him or with David Baird the managing director. Steve Kuntze, their project director came in to the work later.

We had a done deal, subject to legal documentation.

6
The legal contracts

When we agreed with the Receiver for the Metropolitan Police the amount that we would pay as the premium for the head lease of the property we also agreed heads of terms for the contract. We tried to obtain a lock-out agreement from the Receiver (preventing him negotiating with anyone else) but this was not forthcoming, and so we had no way of preventing him negotiating with someone else during the ensuing months. Our preferred private sector partner commitment by London Police Education did not necessarily commit the Receiver.

At this time we were asked to indicate who would be the leaseholder As soon as Salmon Harvester were selected by Bow Street Partners we introduced them to the Police and nominated the Company as funders and developers of the property, but not the museum. The Police indicated that that Company was acceptable to them and this started a lengthy process of contract negotiation between four parties, the Receiver (later succeeded by the Metropolitan Police Authority), Salmon Harvester Properties Ltd., Bow Street Partners Ltd., and the Inner London Magistrates Courts Service which had a right of way running across the Police Station yard.

We had also four other contracts to consider. Lawyers for Bow Street Partners Ltd.'s drafted an agreement with Salmon Harvester Properties Ltd. to define and protect our business relationship. London Police Education Ltd. produced a draft Endorsement Agreement giving rights and responsibilities to Bow Street Partners as creators and operators of the museum. In turn, Bow Street Partners asked Heritage Projects Ltd. for its contract proposal for its management of the museum, although it was agreed that this was not going to be signed as a contract until finance was available to proceed with the museum fit out – an event which was not achieved. Lastly, Bow Street Partners agreed to contract with my consultancy, known as Thorburns, to take forward the design of the museum as this would simplify the management of the finances and specialist consultants needing to be brought together for this work.

The property contract

At first sight the property contract seemed to be the easiest to conclude because it is familiar ground for commercial property lawyers. In practice it took a very long time to agree the details. One of the reasons for the slow progress was the attitude of the Magistrates to the proposal, which is explained in Chapter 22. For many months everything was on hold whilst their agreement was being sought. Another delaying factor arose from the need for Salmon Harvester to check out a wide variety of relatively detailed matters which had not been discussed at Heads of Terms stage. These included the terms under which they could buy the freehold of the property if ever it came onto the market.

By May 2000, a year after we started, the contract was almost ready to be signed, but the Receiver decided that instead of signing it during the last weeks before handing over his responsibilities to the new Metropolitan Police Authority it should be held back for its approval and support. Although no changes were made to the documents as a result of this, it delayed endorsement for another seven frustrating months as the new body was not familiar with its own organisation and priorities. With hindsight the many months of delays then were fatal to the scheme because the Receiver had wider powers than the Authority.

The contract we signed was a conditional agreement for lease of the property which also committed Salmon Harvester to a development agreement with the Metropolitan Police Authority and the leaseback of the premises to be used for the museum. In turn Bow Street Partners agreed to take the sub-underlease of these premises from the Authority. Lastly, Salmon Harvester agreed to lease to the Greater London Magistrates Courts Authority the secure van dock it was building for them as part of the new building works.

The conditional nature of the Agreement for Lease allowed the project to be dropped if the need to protect the rights of daylight or sunlight for the adjacent properties made it unprofitable, or if a satisfactory planning permission could not be obtained. Before Salmon Harvester could be satisfied on these two matters it had to pay for a large amount of professional work wholly at its own risk. I doubt that many readers will realise just how high such expenditure can be, particularly if a full public inquiry is needed. It explains why the developer was so careful about every detail in his contract.

The Agreement for Lease required that Salmon Harvester and Bow Street Partners apply for planning permission and conduct their negotiations on this with all speed. Signing took place in January 2001. In anticipation of this a project management team led by Steve Kuntze, Project Director of Salmon Developments, had already started work.

The two-company agreement

The property contract did not oblige either of us to fit out the museum but the planning permission was expected to contain a condition that this was done before the offices could be occupied. Therefore, Salmon Harvester was dependant upon our doing this, and had a contract with us under which they would provide the money against invoices when required. The Police were told about this contract and were promised that the money would all be used for the museum, but they were not a signatory.

This contract also provided for us to be paid at once for the professional work on the project which had already been done, a sum of around £200,000, and further payments for work done when the Head Lease was concluded. At the time it was very difficult to know how profitable the development would be, and Bow Street Partners negotiated a 20% share of any profit over 15% of the total capital expenditure – which gave us a notional equity stake in its success and a nice bonus had we been lucky. It was intended to motivate us to help maximise property profit.

All of this was going to be a cost to the developer which was factored in to its development appraisals. Except for the profit share it was a fixed cost with no provision for inflation. The rental income the developer would obtain from Bow Street Partners via the Metropolitan Police Authority was index-linked but this was part of a draft tenancy agreement.

The Endorsement Agreement

London Police Education Ltd. was going to endorse the museum and provide Bow Street Partners with its advice and many exhibits. In return it wanted us to pay it an income – as it had none – and accept a veto over the staff and sub-contractors we employed. It would obviously be very embarrassing for the Police if we employed someone whom they were investigating for fraud!

The charity purported to represent the Metropolitan Police Service and the City of London Police Service whose artefacts and other resources they were committing on behalf of the two Police Forces.. Given that it had no resources of its own, we asked for and received assurances that these bodies were equally committed although we never actually saw the contracts. Later we heard that they were described as "service level agreements" which is a term I have never heard before and do not understand. What is clear is that the Endorsement Agreement was not linked in any legal way to the property contracts we had signed, and that this had some detrimental effect upon our position when things went wrong. With hindsight I think that our lawyers might have been able to link them in some way for our protection had they been asked to do so.

THE LEGAL CONTRACTS

The Endorsement Agreement was signed in May 2000. There was no provision for it to be revised or revoked and it remained in existence as long as the two signatories existed. I tried to get it transferred to another property when we lost Bow Street but the Metropolitan Police prevented this happening for some reason I never discovered, and eventually did not pursue.

The management agreement

Management agreement for leisure enterprises normally require that the owner of the enterprise pays all fixed and variable costs and receives all incomes, and this was no exception. This includes staff costs. Heritage Projects had a detailed formula for budgeting these costs, to which we had to commit. The difficult areas are the decisions upon refurbishment plans and other periodic expenditure, the type and quantity of stock to be carried in the shop, the arrangements for promoting functions and events effectively, the marketing budget and the level of entry charges. Whilst Heritage Projects, the police and Bow Street Partners shared common objectives we could see that there would be continuing differences over these matters which would have to be re-negotiated at least once a year.

To maintain our respective negotiating strengths we agreed that the management contract would run for five years, and that Heritage Projects Ltd., would receive a substantial share of our profits. It seemed to me that our prospects of taking home much money ourselves were quite slim unless we could really push the numbers up towards the limits of the capacity of the building. From experience elsewhere I knew that in-house management is too dependant upon finding the right personalities for key jobs for it to be a sensible alternative. We must pay for good and reliable management.

For the moment we accepted, after some alterations, the heads of terms put to us by the Company and did not complete the contract.

The consultancy agreement

The contract between Bow Street Partners and Thorburns was a simple agreement for consultancy services and presented no problems.

7
London's communities

The next thing we needed to do was to find out what was the real agenda for the Police. Large public bodies do not spend as much time and effort at senior level as these people had done just in order to tell the public about the history of their organisation. There were undoubtedly some specific messages they wanted to get across to the public. It was easy to understand that they might not want to tell us about these messages because their intent might backfire if it was known about by some of the public. But I wanted to know.

When I started to probe Alan Moss about this, in an indirect fashion, he mentioned community policing. Knowing that there were public concerns about racism within the Metropolitan Police Force and that it was a challenge to police some racial groups, I asked if he was talking about ethnic communities. He did not confirm this, but from then on I was quite sure that the ethnic issue was a main reason for the museum. I also concluded that both the police and the ethnic minorities had something to learn. But all of this may have been in my mind, for it was never confirmed! Since the events of 9/11 and the identification within these communities of criminals and religious extremists attitudes seem to have changed both within the police and the majority of the public.

However, Alan Moss did make clear that he wanted to tell people about community policing issues. He would like to use the museum to discuss different views of priorities for communities. He was not talking only of ethnic groupings. Religious community groupings such as Jews might feature and maybe cultural groups such as the Irish. He asked me about showing a map of the location of London's communities. I found the information and became enthusiastic about the suggestion as it was interesting in itself, particularly to geographers like me.

Writing to me some months after we had been selected to carry forward the project Alan Moss said that

"One of the principles behind policing a society with minimum force and with consent of the public is that there should be communication and understanding about how the public perceive the Service. Talking to Neighbourhood Watch groups and other community organisations helps to determine the things which should be improved (eg victim support, better information about progress of investigations, better channels of communication about suspicious behaviour, and so on) It is just as much a matter of mutual understanding regardless of whether one is dealing with a specialist interest group, a minority, or a prosperous suburb. It is not unlike any other organisation providing a service and finding out about its customers.

Some communities are keen to retain their own culture and identity within the UK, sometimes because the general morality and ethics of London can be seen to be very poor compared to the more structured, religious, rural or authoritarian communities from which some of them originate. So the police officers on community relations work will often explain the differences which exist in London, and how to make use of the Police Service systems and procedures. Otherwise crimes and incidents can go unreported. Or minority groups feel that the Police are prejudiced against them when in reality it is sometimes the legal system or the law which is different from their expectations.

An example could be, for instance, how racist graffiti or comments in the street are dealt with under the law. It has only been recently that racist intent has been formally specifically catered for as an aggravating feature of what would otherwise not be priority criminal investigations.

There is also a point about mutually respecting cultural diversity with equal commitment to society, and the Police Service's obligation to give equal service to all sections of society, in so far as resources allow.

Community policing is delegated local police arrangements which allow a certain amount of latitude in concentrating upon what the local population regard as priorities which might be quite different from neighbouring places. The importance is the quality of communication about what is happening, suspicious behaviour and information against law breakers, all of which makes policing more effective.

It is also important that there is good cooperation between different agencies such as Social Services, Housing, Probation, Health Authorities and so on, all of whom are likely to have different boundaries, and to be retrenching into concentrating only on core activities because of shortage of resources. Mutual cooperation can give an overall better long term service, especially where there are areas where each agency perceives chronic problems of crime, poverty etc. There is a stereotyped distinction between a soft community orientated approach as distinct from a harder law enforcement approach. Some officers do get confused and try to be social workers, or seem to think that one end of the stereotype scale is more important than the other."

[When I was working on The Beat I did not question this way of consulting on local priorities. Now that I have more time to think I see it as controversial. It is unsafe to assume that people of like ethnic origin who do not feel threatened will group into a community at all. Their spokesmen may speak only for themselves. There may be different factions within an ethnic group. It is also unsafe to assume that the majority of the public will feel themselves competent to form any view about police priorities. Town planners face similar problems when engaging in public participation (which is what they call it). Those of the people who respond are sometimes very unrepresentative but react badly when their views are not accepted.]

It is well known that immigrants bring energy and ambition to London, which helps its economy, its arts, and its vibrancy. They are not a new phenomena as they have been arriving since at least Roman times both from abroad and from the provinces. Black immigrants are recorded from the sixteenth century but some probably came earlier. Sir Thomas de Veil, the Magistrate who started policing in Bow Street, was the son of a Huguenot immigrant minister from Lorraine who arrived more than three hundred years ago. Bow Street Police Station held for a long time the Aliens Registration Office. It is part of the building's history.

Our research showed that there are about 400 different languages spoken by people who live in London. Some of these people live close together in communities where the English culture does not dominate. A greater number live amidst the English and often want to become as English as possible. Some people look different because of their skin colour, hair or physique, others look like English people and only appear distinctive when they speak, or eat different kinds of food. Without them London would be a very different city.

Because the public does not know much about these matters the museum would need to put into perspective the special policing problems that immigrants and their offspring can cause. It is obvious that many new arrivals in the city, be they business people, refugees from persecution, illegal economic immigrants, students, or long term visitors, must come from places where the role and behaviour of the police is very different from that in Britain. This will include places where the police have the job of suppressing dissent or maintaining a ruling group with as much force as they think expedient.

Alongside new residents in London we would be welcoming tourists from abroad, some of whom would have had very different police experiences from our own. They might include policemen from other types of regime. There was plenty of opportunity to succeed or fail in communicating with all these different people.

I thought that the differences between countries in the status or role of the police provided me with an uncontroversial and easily understood basis for explaining the subject matter to my team without suggesting to them that the police seemed to be particularly interested in ethnic community policing. I used it often.

Of course differences between communities can be cultural, language, ethnic, economic, religious, and so forth. Allegations of institutional racism had made the Metropolitan Police very sensitive on these matters. We would need to understand the impact of what we were doing and saying in relation to different communities. That meant that we needed their advice and suggestions.

I thought it best to make direct contact with ethnic community representatives rather than approach them through the existing contacts of the Police, which might not be at all representative. If we were to discover what was helpful to these people we needed to show that when it came to content of the museum we were neither simply putting across the police view, nor promulgating anti-police sentiments. I found my contacts through professional or academic friends. This line led to initial Police alarm, but my contacts were checked out and found acceptable. However, the Police asked that we did not confine ourselves to the views of any one group.

Discussions with these contacts had barely begun but we found that different ethnic groups all relate to the English but not to one another. For instance some wanted to be fully integrated with English culture, to become English before very long, whilst others wanted to maintain their cultural distinctiveness whilst living in England. Political leaders may take a view upon which end of the spectrum they prefer to aim for. Unless the law decrees otherwise, we assumed that policing methods ought to be adapted sensitively to the whole spectrum as well as the different origins of the people. This is not easy.

As museum operators we did not think it useful to go very far into this. Nor should we take any view ourselves of community differences. We just needed to ensure that we could make our show relevant to everyone and effectively communicate its content.

BCCF BLACK CHRISTIAN CIVIC FORUM, UK
promoting citizenship, pursuing justice

SUSTAINABILITY AGENDA FOR MULTI-ETHNIC COMMUNITY POLICING – UNRAVELLING THE MYSTERY FROM WITHIN THE HISTORIC BOW STREET POLICE STATION, COVENT GARDEN.

Sustaining a uniquely complex multi-ethnic, multi-faith and multi-cultural Community Policing, remains at the heart of the Local Agenda 21 Action Plans with policies designed to resolve and diffuse the prevailing confidence crisis situation between the Police and Public, particularly the people from the disadvantaged Black and Ethnic Minority Community.

Recent publication of Sir William Macpherson 350-page report on Stephen Lawrence Case, delivered a scathing verdict on Scotland Yard's handling of the investigation into the murder of the black teenager. The New Labour >vernment has reacted by announcing measūres in the law to eradicate racism in public life. The Prime Minister Tony Blair said: "We should confront as a nation honestly the racism that still exists within our society. We should find within ourselves the will to overcome it."

The Met failed to investigate the murder properly. That failure the Inquiry Chairman says, was due to an inability to provide a 'Professional Service' to ethnic minorities. He provides his definition of Institutionalised racism... a collective failure of an organisation to provide an appropriate and professional service to people because of their colour, culture and ethnic origin.

Sustainable development practitioners perceive the unfortunate incidents as an unusual problem with feasible solutions in the maxim... tting back to the basics on Community rolicing. Bow Street Police Station depicts the past, present and future symbol for understanding the need, including the practicality and value of policing the people.

Professional Policing of London was initially organised by the Bow Street Magistrates and the arrangement gave way to the Metropolitan Police Service that came into existence in 1829 under the then Home Secretary, Sir Robert Peel. The location is therefore of great historical significance. The building is listed Grade II, and has a front facade which is of considerable architectural interest. It will be redeveloped to create a place which will educate the public in an interesting and entertaining way about policing and related issues. It will use modern interactive exhibition techniques, with particular emphasis upon capturing the imagination of the young.

Visitors will enjoy experiences of what it is like to be a police officer, of how problems are solved, and how best to cope with the unexpected. They will discover which past incidents have shaped the way policing is carried out and see some of the equipment used in the past and those proposed for the future. The history of the present London Police will be presented in an interesting fashion that is not offensive or inflammatory to the public. Cultural diversity has always brought and created prejudices and misunderstandings and has contributed to policing difficulties at many times over the last 160 years. The project will assist towards London Capital City, being a centre of excellence for advancing the art of community policing.

The museum-type development will be designed, constructed and managed to attract and keep happy a wide range of people paying reasonable entry charges. The development will incorporate a few shop-type uses such as a restaurant, sandwich bar and wine bar which will open into the evening to add to the liveliness of the Covent Garden Area.

Public trust and police confidence remains the fundamental concept for project success. The main funding will be from the private sector. Non-commercial objectives could be backed by available public grants. Funding generally excludes direct sources of finance by the Metropolitan Police Service and the City of London Police. Given the scale of the project and its unique qualities for education, entertainment and tourist attractions in a high profile location of Covent Garden, the social and economic benefits are unquestionable.

Planning of the project coincides with the New Millennium. This is a natural milestone in the development history for building that represents 19th, 20th and 21st Century Community Policing

Using the theme of London policing, The Bow Street Project will combine entertainment, education and historic reference to attract a wide audience. It will also be an information centre and meeting point. As a facility for community interaction with police education, careers staff and interested parties, it should offer some solution to racial and social tensions.

This is a private sector project at no burden to the taxpayer. It deserves a support from the parties. It will make good use of an otherwise redundant historical building and provide wider benefit beyond its commercial redevelopment and museum attraction. It is a natural evolution of this building from its use, location and symbolism.

Suggestions for names of project when completed, will be encouraged from school children in and around the Greater London Area.

The Black Christian Civic Forum (BCCF)-UK will be asking church members to offer support to the project. What matters to this Forum is that the scheme is sustainable on its own commercial standing but in particular that it may help to resolve conflict. It will achieve this through its educational messages to foster better community relations by proper understanding of community policing, race relations and citizenship for all.

For more information about the Bow Street Project, contact:

FALANA ASSOCIATES

Yomi Falana
Falana Associates (Consulting Environmental Managers)
Albert Buildings 49 Queen Victoria Street
London EC4N 4SA
Tel: +44 (0) 171 248 1155   Fax: +44 (0) 171 248 4455
E-mail: falanaassociates@x-stream.co.uk

Reverend Abraham Lawrence
Secretary-General, BCCF(UK)
c/o Mile End New Testament Church of God
Lichfield Road, Bow, London E3
Tel: 0181-473 6771   Fax: 0181-480 7914
E-mail: rakeshra@aol.com

We thought that it might be hard to get people from some communities to come to the museum at all. We thought that suggesting these people needed to be 'educated' would be counter-productive. We needed to give priority to finding ways of appealing to them and avoid offending them. Hence it was important to focus on this aspect of practical policing.

A key person in this was Yomi Falana a young professional planner and valuer in London whose father was a Nigerian policeman and who was closely involved with the Black Christian Civic Forum, a body advising the London Assembly and Mayor. He brought in Ashis Choudhury from an Indian community and I met with several others. They were all strongly supportive of our proposals. We very much welcomed the leaflet put out (without consulting us) by the BCCF which is reproduced opposite.

As a result of their efforts Westminster City Council received letters of support for the museum from community groups as diverse as:-

London Civic Forum,
Pakistan Christian World Organisation,
Caring for Carers association,
The African Families Foundation,
Krishna Yoga Mandir,
Black Cultural Archives,
African Community Forum,
African Youth Initiative,
London Muslim Centre,
Davish Enterprise Development Centre Ltd.,
Genuine Empowerment of Mothers in Society,
Pensioners of Southwark,
Aimex International,
GALOP
African & Caribbean Voices Association,
Brent Indian Association,
Hampstead (Quaker) Monthly Meeting,
Anglo Jewish Association,
Friends of Grenada Hospital Association,
The Paralegal Charity,
W.F.Carers Association,
Isle of Dogs Community Foundation,
Nunsbrook Community Group.

Some police literature has to be published in foreign languages if it is to reach its targets and I was shown examples of this. At first we thought that this would mean multiple languages should be used in The Beat but as we went forward we found this was impractical. It was better to minimise use of language to convey messages.

We were setting up a business. Whether it was in our commercial interest to concern ourselves with ethnic diversity is a moot point. It might have cost us more than the extra visitors brought in. I did not know, but it was in the best interest of London to avoid being penny pinching on the matter.

8
The customers

Continuing our businessman's focus we began to think about the types of visitor we would be attracting, and their preferences. There are a number of attractions in tourist cities like London which visitors "must see" in order to enjoy the prestige of being able to talk about them when they return home. For London schoolchildren The Beat would easily fall in to that category. It would be the same for those working in police services. But for others one would need to be both clever and lucky to attract such a cachet. Potential visitors would need to be targeted in a precise and determined way and we set about working out how we would do this. We selected a number of principal targets, as follows: -

Schoolchildren

The Police Service was particularly keen to bring young people in, presumably so that they can learn about the police early on and without prejudice. The total number of children of any one age in London schools is about 90,000. It is reasonable to assume that most schools will want each school child to make one visit with his or her class whilst at school. They will be attracted by direct marketing to teachers, with the help of the local police.

Young people from overseas

This is quite a large group of visitors to London and South East England, including school parties, back-packers and language students. Some of the young people may be seriously interested in British policing, because of family connections or career intentions, whilst others are simply curious, or maybe are brought here for their own good by their guides or teachers.

Young people from the provinces

This is an even larger group of potential visitors but there is so much else of interest for them to do in London that only a small proportion is likely to be attracted. They can be targeted through coach companies and advertising.

Potential police service recruits

Those who are being considered for recruitment to train as police officers, security staff, or civilian support staff would be brought here to learn more about the work through specially devised programmes. These are easily targeted.

Police trainees from within this country

This is a nice steady market which will know about the place in advance and can also be offered special programmes.

Police and security personnel and their families

Policemen, retired policemen, military policemen, security forces and civilian support staff, with or without their families, may visit during leisure outings or when on business in London. Some will be from overseas and need translation services.

Adult coach parties from overseas or the provinces

The diversity of interest that we will provide would be attractive to tour operators with time to fill in, but there is strong competition for this market.

Families with children

Some children who have visited with their teachers may want to come here again with their siblings, parents or grandparents. There will be other children, possibly from the Home Counties, who have not been on a school visit. This is where competitive pressures will be strongest, and cost-effective marketing quite difficult.

Media and tourism executives

These will be especially demanding visitors and hence noticeable. They will also provide a means for attracting others, and for spreading the resources of the attraction more widely.

Other adults

Again competition will be strong in this sector, but the total number of adult residents and visitors to London with time to spare is high. A large sector of this market is retired, with time to spare. There are many opportunities to market to London visitors as part of packages and through hotels or transport companies.

Participants in parties and functions

The venue will also be uniquely interesting and attractive for corporate entertainment, office parties, and other private events. Organisers of such events can be approached directly and jointly with suitable catering firms.

Many of these targets would be attracted through word of mouth or special promotions. Word of mouth recommendations come from satisfaction in the way the place is managed, its value for money, and the interest generated by its content - probably in that order for most people. Promotion rests upon the ability to reach likely people with an attractive message, frequent reminders, and special reasons for coming on a particular day - so that the sale is actually closed. It follows that the projections of visitor numbers below are substantially dependent upon the chosen operator rather than the product being offered.

All the numbers assume that pricing will give good value, and that the average stay would be about one and a half hours. These projections indicate that space should ideally be designed to take peak numbers equivalent to 550,000 in order to prevent people being put off by overcrowding. Using normal standards this equates to about 2,200 sq.m. excluding retailing or catering provision. However, when we had finished work on the design of the building we did not have enough space for this. At peak times the admissions would have to be controlled to prevent overcrowding. It follows that total maximum numbers would be less than the figures suggest.

	Total per year	
	Min '000	*Max* '000
School children	80	100
Young people from overseas	30	50
Young people from the provinces	25	35
Potential police service recruits	15	30
Police trainees	5	10
Police or security personnel and families	35	50
Adult coach parties	20	40
Families	60	90
Media and tourism executives	10	25
Other adults	80	115
Private evening events	<u>10</u>	<u>15</u>
Totals	370	550
	(unconstrained)	

We needed to know more about the requirements of teachers and non-English cultures. Police officers responsible for school liaison may influence the desire to visit The Beat but the decision rests with the teachers. They will be concerned about the availability of a schoolroom and other specific facilities and the problems of maintaining discipline. As professionals used to learning methods they would need to be consulted during the design process. Our intention was to appoint a consultative group of London teachers who would help us develop features, and programmes within the features, so that they appeal to, and are good for, children of all ages. Thus we would become customer orientated towards these gatekeepers for the learning classes.

Similarly, in order to attract people from cultural groups who are not English, as discussed in the last chapter, we needed to avoid or handle very carefully the matters upon which they are especially sensitive. We also needed to know what would have special appeal to them. Such information might not be available within our teams in the way it is with the English culture and to fill this gap we intended to identify several individuals familiar within each of the main cultures to advise us. The Black Christian Civic Forum seemed a good but not exclusive place to start to find these people.

Whilst I was sifting through some papers I had put by, I had the good luck to re-read an interesting talk by Christine MacNulty of Taylor Nelson, reporting upon research which she carried out in the '80's. She had divided people into seven types, regardless of an individual's age and cultural background. It was clear from what she said that the attitudes and interests of the types are so different as to present a design problem for visitor attractions.

To draw the attention of our design team to this knowledge I prepared the following notes to be attached to their briefing. I hasten to add that Christine MacNulty has not been consulted and is in no way responsible for my pragmatic interpretation of her work. It is a long time since I spoke with her but I think she may be happy to see some use of her work and recognition of its importance.

The notes I wrote down about the seven types of people as applied to our project are as follows.

Average people who will probably comprise about a fifth of the total visitors, but fewer from the lower social classes. They will come with their families in well planned visits and will not be

politically or socially aware. Their attitudes will mostly depend upon their families' reactions. These average people reject change and will be wary of technology. They are careful with money. They will want an increase in officer numbers on the beat.

Buyers, mainly women, will be another fifth of the visitors. These will want to spend in the shop - for large ticket items if these are sufficiently prestigious. They will often come in tour groups. They are not very concerned about social and political issues, but are open to new ideas and self improvement for the longer term.

Experimentalists will form a large proportion of the corporate groups being young, affluent and interested in new immersive and active experiences especially with high technology. They live fast so will not linger. Attractive gadgets will sell to them in the shop. They are liberal minded but not very aware socially or politically. They will make up about one seventh of our visitors.

Convention-orientated people with the protestant work ethic will naturally support the police and will welcome the educational and informative nature of the show. They will come with their families or schools, and will be politically and socially aware. They are likely to number about one sixth of the visitors.

Self-explorers are better educated and work long hours. They may be affluent but not acquisitive, and are likely to have liberal attitudes. They support pressure groups and may have strong views about the police. They want information and are confident but will not succumb to advertising, or to the beliefs of others. They are open to new experiences. About one fifth of the visitors are likely to be in this type. (I, and my daughters fall into this category)

Aimless young people are normally very hostile to the police, and chauvinistic. They are likely to be unemployed and most will not be able to afford to come to The Beat or will have little enthusiasm to do so. They are likely to form gangs which are violent. These people see change and flexibility as threats whilst they need order and a rigid set of rules. We might get a few hundred of these people in any year, but they could be in very hostile gangs.

Traditional working class people are not interested in broadening their experiences and do not have money for this, but they like escapist activities such as TV or pub. Some may come on a chance spree and some with schools parties. They are disillusioned with all institutions including the Police. They fear change. Total numbers might be a few thousand a year. This might be increased by a truly immersive experience that is not too advanced.

The conclusions

From this analysis we drew the conclusion that the museum should be strong on the following:-
- The high prestige of a visit to this place,
- Special things which the affluent can buy.
- Unusual experiences in which not more than one third of visitors can get immersed as many will not be interested.
- Familiar experiences which are reasonably informative

- New information for those who are already well informed
- Information for those who have much less knowledge and interest in knowledge
- A neutral attitude to innovation and technology
- The confident certainty of a stable policing system that the police should exude
- Easy involvement in everything - no task or hurdles too hard to be overcome.
- The mixing of such different types of people could lead to some tensions that will be less if some areas are more suited to one type of person than another.

I have often wondered what those with great enthusiasm for the museum would have made of this realism about public interest and response. And I wonder what the down-to-earth policeman would have thought about some of the visitors. Firm steering would have been needed to achieve these featured characteristics amidst the turbulence of the detailed design process and especially when budgets for each feature were being squeezed to avoid over-runs.

> *"I handled a telescopic police baton the other day. It is surprising how memorable just that simple activity was, despite being otherwise immersed in a high tech world."*
> *Will Baker 2/10/00*

9
The Police perspective

In their way, the London Police were also going to be a customer, and a very fussy one. London Police Education Ltd. was not the designers' client but I would have to ensure that its Board Members did not dislike what the design team were offering visitors, for they could remove official Police endorsement. Whilst their doing that would not have closed down the museum it would have kept us out of the "must see" list of tourist attractions and deprived us of some of the schools as customers. We might have had to do without the objects on loan to us from the police which would have left us very short of things to display.

We had agreed to pay a royalty to London Police Education related to the number of visitors over 225,000 a year, our supposed break-even point. We expected that as the charity had no premises of their own it would use this money for educational activities centred at The Beat that were of a kind which our commercial objectives precluded us from offering. These activities might include running discussion sessions and providing volunteer retired police officers to help show people around and answer questions. Thus the charity might be involved on a daily basis in the experiences we offered.

In addition to pleasing London Police Education we wanted individuals working in any role within or for the Police Services to like what we were doing. We wanted them to feel that it was their place as much as ours. After fifteen years it would be. That was in our contracts. To help with this we spoke to a variety of police people quite informally.

We met with the Friends of the Historical Museum who were very interested and supportive. I feel sad that they were ultimately let down.

Our meeting with the committee of the London branch of the Association of Retired Police Officers did not go so well. They objected strongly to the kind of museum London Police Education was proposing and we were providing. They wanted something like a regimental museum for the two Police Forces. After I had explained to the committee the agreed reasons for proposing something other than a regimental museum, including the emphasis on educating children and the impossibility of breaking even financially with the operation of such a museum, they took their concerns to the highest level of the Police. They did not prevail. I asked their committee to let me know what specifically they would like us to include but they did not reply with any suggestions. I hoped that later discussions would win them around. My guess is that most of their membership would have come anyway, if only to enjoy criticising us!

The official police view of content

Right from the beginning I was conducting a continuing dialogue with Alan Moss about the content of the museum in accordance with the consultation process to which we were committed. His first paper was reviewed by London Police Education before it was sent to me in December 1998, just after we were selected. He called it the "design brief" and it brought together points made in our early talks. I was cautious about trying to work from this as I felt that some suggestions would not work. Two months later I wrote a rather different document on the same subject and circulated it to Alan and others for discussion, including the design steering committee we had established by then. I don't think this paper was ever seen by the Board of London Police Education and Alan responded only on selected points.

It had emerged early on that the Police thought that people visiting the place would learn and remember what they were told, as if they were in the class room of a Grammar School. My more cautious assumption was that visitors might obtain a benign view of the police from what we said but would really only learn from their own experiences whilst visiting the place. This realism links with my view that many of the people who avoid or are hostile to the police do not take readily to formal ways of education. It seems to me that this applies regardless of intelligence, race, class creed or gender. Of course, philosophies of teaching are not a subject upon which I have any expertise, but I have watched large numbers of visitors trying to enjoy and comprehend visitor attractions – and read survey reports upon what they say when questioned.

As we proceeded with our thinking we more and more came to see that we could produce experiences that were emotional rather than intellectual. In this we were unlike a science centre. At about this time I was particularly intrigued by a book which Will Baker gave me which reviewed recent research into emotions. The book indicated that an intense emotional experience lasting less than a minute would probably influence behaviour and attitude for the rest of ones life. In policing, there are lots of emotional experiences for both the public and the police officer. That was the way to put over our messages, to get the place talked about, and to be better than the study books or the Bobby in the classroom. How could we do it?

The Police were keen to impart information, but I wanted them to remember that we were, after all, producing a show that one had to visit in person. Information that could readily be used in schools would be left for the Virtual Museum to handle. Only in this way could we be comprehensive in content. The Beat on its own was not able to take a look at all aspects of policing London. Our selection of content would be quite subjective.

In one paper Alan wrote as follows:-

> "The museum should require and help young people not only to develop a sense of the importance of good citizenship, but also to undertake responsible decision- making and understand cultural differences. The experience will also hopefully sow the seeds of commitment to make the capital a safer place in the future. Younger people should be able to see the effects of people making a contribution to the community and other aspects of good citizenship.
>
> "It should explore the role of policing in London from the early days through to the present and in to the future, using an enjoyable but thought provoking mix of exhibits, and modern interactive techniques that allow experience of real life situations in controlled conditions."

To explain an alternative approach I sent Alan a paper by our interactives consultant Ian Russell in which he advised:-

> "Visitors must never have any sense that they are being 'told' a prepared message. Through sensitively designed interactions, they will be 'soaking up' appropriate feelings, attitudes and values while experiencing 'incidents' alongside policemen.
>
> "A policeman is the ultimate authority-figure, with all the resulting emotions this engenders in the visitor. Direct, formal, thumbs-behind-lapels statements are unlikely to be the most effective means of touching visitors positively at any deep level. Low status figures must be used constantly to communicate anything more than the most basic factual messages. The victim of a crime, or the sweating, anxious-looking policeman on the interactive screen who turns to the camera and asks 'What the heck should I do now?"

It was with Ian's comments in my mind that I set down for the approval of London Police Education the ten messages that I thought we should be putting across.

These are:
1. Policing is essential for all human communities
2. At the core of sound policing is using common sense, knowledge and experience to guide or restrain people to behave acceptably and legally.
3. British policing does not impose state control over citizens, although it restrains felons and rioters.

4. Different types of problems are encountered by policemen on the beat. The actions needed to solve them also differ.
5. Most types of policing situations have occurred before and will occur again.
6. Knowledge of past events improves policing.
7. Good communications helps policing to be more efficient.
8. Forensics and other technology leads to more efficient policing.
9. The police need help from the public.
10. The police are human and not infallible.

Alan Moss took these messages to the Board with his interpretation, and sent me the paper which appears on the next four pages.

It seemed to me that this paper raised significant questions about what we could and should convey to the typical visitor (and even to our designers) but I decided to see what 'came out in the wash' rather than to pursue agreement of content in the abstract. For this reason we did not include this paper in our briefing for designers but intended to pick up on points as and when there was opportunity to do so.

Basic police work

Members of the team made visits to some of the specialist units of the Metropolitan Police and the City of London Police to find out what they did. It was after one of these visits that I said to Alan that obviously not all of the police are specialists like detectives, traffic police, dog-handlers, river police or mounted police. I asked; "What is the basic task of policing?"

"What do you do when you go on duty?"

He replied that it was deciding where to place your officers. That led to one of the proposed features that will tell people more about why there is not always a policeman at one's beck and call than could ever be conveyed by speeches or writings. The visitor will try to place his officers.

THE POLICE PERSPECTIVE

Version 3 - 22.12.2000

MESSAGES WITHIN "THE BEAT"

Starting from Andrew Thorburn's 10 messages, as presented to London Police Education Ltd on 4th May, I have tried to reconcile the ideas with the more conventional concepts and language used within the Service.

The importance is firstly that the general philosophy of the Museum should accord with Police Service thinking; and secondly, that important issues are not omitted.

The ideas need to be introduced to the public in easily understood forms and language. Some ideas are more easily grouped together than others.

THE TEN MESSAGES	COMMENTS
1 Policing is essential for all human communities.	There need to be rules by which society governs itself. Some communities can organise themselves without formal policing arrangements, but the more disparate and loose knit the community becomes, the less likely it is that there will be the same degree of commonly held and naturally self-enforcing norms of behaviour. The existence of recognised authority figures, a system of discipline and recognised norms of behaviour are some of the factors which make communities easier, rather than harder to police. School pupils are sometimes asked to imagine their community without a Police Service. A good place to start.
3 **British policing does not impose state control over citizens, but it must uphold the law.**	This is a constitutional and historical point, allied to *Policing Style* and *Accountability*. The constitutional arrangements bring the Police under the accountability of the law. The Constitution does not give the Police Service any more information and access to powers than necessary and does not give the Government political control over police operations. The City of London Police has had a Local Police Authority to whom it is responsible since 1839, but the Police Authority for the Metropolitan Police has been the Home Secretary since its foundation right up until the formation of the Metropolitan Police Authority on 3rd July 2000. Officers act as citizens with a few extra powers, but with the strength of a disciplined organisation, the head of which is accountable in general terms, but not in individual operational cases, to a Police Authority, and in some

Version 3 - 22.12.2000

	respects to the Home Secretary. The doctrine of *Minimum Force* is a manifestation of the Constable's *accountability to the law.* It is not permitted to use force against a citizen unless justified. The way of demonstrating what is, or is not permissible will have to be relevant rather than bland. The Police are *Public Servants* and are drawn into *Policing by Consent,* which means that the Police have to maintain public support in general terms for what they are doing and how they do the job; the Government will not impose an autocratic police state on citizens in a liberal democracy.
9 The police need help from the public	Because of Policing by Consent, the police need to be seen to be *treating people fairly* which means understanding the viewpoint of others, not stereotyping or making false assumptions about people, understanding all parts of the community, including minorities, and policing a diverse city so that all sections of the community and newly arrived people come to respect and support the system for upholding the law for the benefit of everyone. If the police are to uphold the law, they need to know who is committing offences, when and where incidents have occurred, and to be able to bring eye witness evidence to prove cases in a court of law.
2 At the core of sound policing is using common sense, knowledge and experience to guide or restrain people to behave acceptably and legally	*Police discretion* is a crucial aspect of how the police uphold the law, many parts of which are routinely broken by the public. A police officer is likely to be criticised for enforcing the law too rigidly or pedantically. A blind eye, a caution or a prosecution can be more significant than the threat of prosecution. The ultimate responsibility is to *maintain the Queen's Peace,* so that communities should not be roused into antagonism by police tactics against, say, street robberies (cf *Consent and Balance* in the Scarman Report into the 1981 Brixton Riots). Crime reduction tactics can ultimately become controversial as in *Zero Tolerance.* There is also the legal system which operates on a range between *Crime Control and Due Process* (ie at one extreme bearing down on accused offenders with great severity to reduce crime; as against maintaining public confidence in the fairness of the legal process which acknowledges the risk of individuals escaping punishment at the other extreme). *The Statement of Common Purpose and Values*

Version 3 - 22.12.2000

	developed by the Police Service in 1989-90 embodies much of these principles, but there are some underlying tensions not only for *Values*, but also in regard to *Resources and Priorities*. The City of London Police has a Statement of Values, and the MPS has, under Sir John Stevens, dealt with *Mission, Values and Vision* (see later).
4 Different types of problems are encountered by police officers on the Beat. The actions needed to solve them also differ.	The Museum should illustrate a comprehensive range of policing situations, the consequences of making certain sorts of decisions, and how different agencies need to collaborate on solutions in a *Multi-Agency Approach*. Some incidents need specialist assistance from police teams, civil staff or outside contractors (eg special investigators; identification officers, scene examiners, intelligence analysts, explosives officers).
6 Knowledge of past events improves policing **5 Most types of policing situations have occurred before and will occur again**	Historical perspectives are often illuminating. Crises are often dealt with by reference to what happened last time, or by forgetting what occurred earlier. There are a number of examples where riots have occurred previously about job losses or controversial taxes; bombs have been set off by criminal terrorists; trains have crashed; murders have been unsolved amid public clamour (eg Jack the Ripper) and sections of the community perceive themselves unfairly treated by the police (eg Jewish people at the time of Mosley). The capital city has often accommodated the bases of groups who are opposed to other governments in the world because of the very nature of democracy. There are *defining moments* which have variously led to Inquiries, or reviews of policing policy and practices (eg the Willink Commission set up after the Garrett v Eastmond complaint of assault witnessed by Brian Rix the actor; the Maxwell Confait murder case which resulted in the Phillips Royal Commission on Criminal Procedure; Stephen Lawrence; the potential problems of demonstrations near the Houses of Parliament)
7 Good communications help policing to be more efficient.	Communication can be considered at different levels. Communication with, and understanding of the perspectives of, all sections of the community helps to set policing priorities wisely. Communication within the organisation aids leadership and effectiveness. Operational communication by radios and other technology is crucial if response to incidents is to be

8 Forensic Science and other technology leads to better evidence and more efficient policing.	efficient. The Information Systems and Technology revolution transforms the way communication policing is done, and the information rapidly available. Computers help with rapid searching of vehicle number plates to check on whether they are reported stolen or the details of registered keepers. Traffic signals are coordinated throughout London to achieve a better flow than could be achieved by officers on point duty. Personal radios are efficient and flexible for coomunication between any parts of London; Word processors help with reports. The HOLMES computer system contains all details of statements and enquiries for major crime investigations rather than bulky card indices, and so on. Forensic science allows exact identification of suspects through body fluids /DNA, and many other comparison techniques, including calculation of vehicle speeds from skid marks.
10 The Police are human, and not infallible	There is sometimes a balance to be struck between over-use of technology, patrol cars, and systems on one hand, and the human touch of the patrolling officer on the other. The perceptions of the public are governed by the situations in which they see police officers operating, and the human awareness skills are no less important than the organisational systems which support the officer on the beat. Contact with police officers who use discretion wisely can tend to generate more trust and understanding of the human side of police work. The public probably distinguish between individual faults and errors and organisational weaknesses.
	The overall purpose of LPE and the Museum is public education, supported by belief that a better understanding of policing issues, and insights into the problems, will, in the long term, and with effort on both sides, lead to visitors being more likely to help the mission of policing London.

Alan's paper alludes to the Mission Statements of the two Forces, which is as follows.

STATEMENT OF OUR COMMON PURPOSE AND VALUES

The purpose of the Police Service is to uphold the law fairly and firmly; to prevent crime; to pursue and bring to justice those who break the law; to keep the Queen's Peace; to protect, help and reassure the community; and to be seen to do all this with integrity, common sense and sound judgement.

We must be compassionate, courteous and patient, acting without fear or favour or prejudice to the rights of others. We need to be professional, calm and restrained in the face of violence and apply only that force which is necessary to accomplish our lawful duty.

We must strive to reduce the fears of the public and, so far as we can, to reflect their priorities in the action we take. We must respond to well-founded criticism with a willingness to change.

CITY OF LONDON POLICE

OUR VALUES

We are committed to:
- Being sensitive, open and fair
- Ensuring equality of opportunity
- Encouraging participation and consultative management practices
- Acting with integrity, compassion, courtesy and patience

METROPOLITAN POLICE SERVICE
A policing pledge for Londoners (2000)

Mission-
Making London safe for all the people we serve.
We:
- Make places safer.
- Cut crime and the fear of crime.
- Uphold the law

Values -
- Treat everyone fairly
- Be open and honest
- Work in Partnership
- Change to Improve

Vision
To make London the safest major city in the world

Our proposed scenarios or features

In May 2000 three of us met with London Police Education to talk about what the museum would contain. We explained the draft list of 'scenarios' that we might include, and the eight different lines of content, which would probably be shown in each scenario unless this was inappropriate. Subsequently, I received a detailed matrix of notes which explored what information was available and what might be said under each scenario. When I read these notes I felt that they would help our designers but could too easily be taken as briefs for the design of each feature. This would not be good because our analysis of customers had shown we needed a great mix of presentation styles and content to attract people from right across the spectrum. Also, some features might end up looking as if they had been designed by a committee not an individual, and executive control of fit-out would be cumbersome. We had to find a different approach.

Perhaps some of the ideas we explored made London Police Education uneasy. They are people used to being in control. They didn't want a theme park and were not familiar with the dynamics of visitor attractions or with the way visitors might behave. We dealt with this by being careful not to commit ourselves to anything until they had seen what it would be like. As I expected the design to come out much better than they expected I tried to reassure them that our approach would prove to be just what they wanted.

Our subsequent decision was that we should give a designer and his team their heads with a subject and expect them to put their own individuality and experience into issues of presentation, emphasis etc. We needed really creative people to give fresh impetus. I needed to decide who these people were going to be, and to set them some challenging limits and requirements. The overall direction had to be exercised with a selective and light touch. That would motivate them, and give them the feeling that they owned the features they designed. If their features were not better than the others they would be motivated to improve them. Choosing the designers is described in Chapter 15.

10

How policing has changed

One of the most useful notes which Alan Moss gave me included the following summary of changes in policing:-

Crime and the fear of crime from footpads and highwaymen have changed in nature and scale, but not in principle. Gentlemen no longer routinely carry swords and firearms as necessary protection, but some parts of London still feel far less safe than others.

The Constable on beat patrol, on foot, has become relatively rare. Gradually, policing functions have become more specialist, and the officers who would otherwise have been proceeding by foot, are now employed against particular problems. Systems such as Neighbourhood Policing have tried to tie in policing teams more closely to local communities, but these have tended to dissipate when faced with the pressures of providing a response to telephoned emergency calls, and to staff major crime enquiries. Auxiliaries in different forms, such as traffic wardens, school crossing patrols and Community Support Officers create more patrolling visibility on the streets, but there is increasing complexity of the extent of the legal powers held by each.

The Opium Wars, and the laudanum and cocaine of Wilkie Collins and Sir Arthur Conan Doyle have given way to widespread availability of cannabis and other drugs used by a wider set of the population, and a significant proportion of acquisitive crime is fuelled by drug addicts seeking money to feed their drug habits. The pervasive influence of cheap gin is not a problem today, but the behaviour of those who are drunk and disorderly is a continuing problem, and sometimes represents the way in which young British men are seen abroad.

Attitudes have been shaped by events such as Wars. Corporal punishment and instinctive obedience to authority have diminished as the experience of service in the Armed Forces has decreased.

Congestion has changed with the motor car taking over from horse transport. Traffic control has moved from police officers on point duty to computer assisted traffic signals, TV cameras, camera offence detection, and congestion charging systems. The streets are cleaner and better lit, but not necessarily less congested.

The smog is no longer the problem it was.

Local government has changed, and agencies like the Fire Brigade and Ambulance Service have become specialist emergency services. There is not the same need for supervision and licensing of messengers, boot blacks, and pedlars. The Metropolitan Police has been the only agency with pan-London boundaries for much of its history, and is now in the process of becoming much more firmly linked to London Boroughs, particularly with the enhanced Local Authority responsibility for crime prevention under the Crime and Disorder Act 1998, and the position of the Mayor of London, the Greater London Authority and Metropolitan Police Authority. This may make policing policy more likely to be the subject of electioneering.

The working conditions, housing, uniform and equipment of police officers have changed over the years. The wooden truncheon, worn concealed, has been replaced by more efficient instruments which are too large or rigid to be worn inside the uniform. CS gas equipment is now carried routinely, and there are Armed Response Vehicles patrolling on a 24 hour basis to improve the response time to incidents where firearms may be involved. Health and Safety considerations now present specific legislative reasons for Police forces to protect their employees and the traditional relationship of an unarmed officer risking the outcome of a volatile incident by using personal persuasion and personal initiative is fading away. Some less lethal alternatives to firearms have been introduced as the consequences of the use of firearms to resolve conflict situations have become better understood. The doctrine of minimum force still applies to the law governing police actions regardless of the threat. Some situations, eg intercepting suspected suicide bombers, strain the accepted norms and public expectations of the Police service with which they are familiar.

Communication has been transformed by the introduction of the telephone and other modern technology such as mobile telephones and email.

Technology has also transformed crime scene investigation. The beginning of the 20th century brought fingerprints; the 21st century DNA.

Public disorder and demonstrations have less connection with the reform of Parliament, the price of gin and the rights of Catholics; but are just as likely to be caused by threats to employment, and introduction of the poll tax.

Terrorism has involved Irish nationalism for many years of London's history. The technology of explosive devices has become more sophisticated. The developments of international politics are just as likely to be reflected on the streets of London, and Middle Eastern tensions, particularly in the form of suicide bombers, are likely to remain with London for some years.

The role of magistrates and their operational influence over the police has changed from the early days of Bow Street under Thomas de Veil and the Fielding Brothers. Access to the prosecution process is now largely controlled by the Crown Prosecution Service, and lawyers have more involvement than in the past. Capital punishment and transportation were once regular punishments, but both have now been abolished, with a corresponding effect upon the prison population.

Legal procedures have become more formal, particularly since the Police and Criminal Evidence Act 1984. The doctrine of crime control with the risk of alienating the public, or sections of it, by firmer policing, continues to be in tension with due process where the controlling legal procedures are seen to be more important than obtaining a conviction in any one particular case.

People from all over the world continue to arrive and settle in London, largely without major tensions and discrimination, but there are shifting patterns of expectations of public services, and variations in the patterns of the origin of those who are seen to be strangers.

Trade and commerce continues as a prime concern of the capital city which houses the seat of Government, Parliament, the official residence of the Sovereign, and the foreign diplomatic community.

Police Officers in charge of Police Forces have been long-standing professional police officers for 50 years, but the long term effects, and implications of providing the in-depth leadership and technical training are still not so advanced as the arrangements for the Armed Services.

This note was going to be used as we moved on to guide the choice of content for the exhibits and the presentation of historic content. Also, there was more historic information available which had to be used. This related to the police history of Bow Street and the former police station itself. I shall set this out in the next chapter before moving on to a description of the museum we saw emerging from all this conceptual thinking and discussion.

The new Courts (left) and Police Station in 1881

11

Policemen in Bow Street

When you want to attract people to a place it is useful for it to be well known. English people generally know of Bow Street because of the Bow Street Magistrates Court, or the Royal Opera House, or a square on the board game Monopoly, or the Bow Street Runners which were the first British police force. The Court is known because it is frequently mentioned in media reports. It handles high profile cases due to its special status in our legislation - not least as the Court where extradition cases are heard. The square on the Monopoly board is a development site. The inventor of the game did not want to use the names of privately owned sites as locations for the game's property deals. All twelve of the names are of London police stations.

The start of the Bow Street Runners is a more complicated story. Just before the beginning of the Industrial Revolution that made Britain the world's dominant nation for a while, most of the wealth and power in England lay with the big country estates and their aristocratic or royal owners. Mostly, these looked after themselves rather than the general citizenry. They largely financed the army and the church, and as cities like London expanded they controlled the availability of land for building. Bow Street was built on land belonging to the Duke of Bedford who did not sell his estate there until 1920.

London was an unruly city without any policemen as we know them today. There were night watchmen called Charlies who were too weak to be effective. Gentlemen had a responsibility to try and keep order and there were magistrates to hear cases brought before them. Most of the Westminster and Marylebone magistrates were corrupt.

In 1739 or 1740 a magistrate who was unusually honest and was well connected with the church and the army moved his office from Soho into No 4 Bow Street. This property stood on the west side of the Street a few yards south of the original Opera House. The site was recently swallowed by the latest extension of that building. The Duke must have welcomed his new tenant because of the effect he would have upon crime in the neighbourhood.

The magistrate was Capt. Thomas de Veil, (later Sir Thomas) son of an impecunious Huguenot minister who looked after the library in Lambeth Palace. Thomas had joined the army, been commissioned a Captain at eighteen, and seen service in Flanders with William III and later in Portugal. After this he left active service on half pay and by the time he moved his office from Holborn to Bow Street he had been a justice of the peace for ten years and was in his mid-fifties. He had bravely taken on and been attacked by criminal gangs and corrupt justices. His connections and experience enabled him to initiate a high level of justice which has persisted in the Bow Street Magistrates Court ever since.

Sir Thomas's office, No 4, remained in use as a Magistrates Court until 1881, having been extended by the addition of No. 3 in 1812 when a custody suite was built to replace the prisoner accommodation the Magistrates had been renting in the notorious Brown Bear pub opposite. Until 1839 Magistrates Courts and offices were privately owned. After that the Government became the owner. It did not maintain Nos. 3 and 4 very well and by the 1870's the degree of dilapidation of this and the police station on the opposite side of the road made it urgently necessary to find replacements. This was discussed with the Duke of Bedford's agent and a site was found for the rather grand new Court and Police Station opposite the Royal Opera House, of which more later.

This property remained in public ownership until 2005 when the police and the magistrates continued presence in Bow Street regrettably came to an end. At the time this book went to press the Magistrates were still sitting in the building but only on a temporary basis.

Returning to my account of earlier days, when Sir Thomas de Veil died in 1746 his office was occupied by a justice called Poulson for two years and he was then replaced by the 41 year old Sir Henry Fielding (magistrate, author and playwright) who devised the idea of paid permanent magistrates each commanding a small force of permanent constables. His proposed system would be centred on Bow Street Police Office. In 1753 he obtained some money to set up a full time foot patrol of seven men who had previously served as parish constables for a year. This patrol did not wear uniform.

Sir Henry was unable to obtain permanent financing for his patrol and it was soon disbanded only to be revived a year or two later by his blind brother John Fielding, later Sir John, who succeeded Sir Henry as Chief Magistrate when he died in 1754 and continued in office until 1780 when he retired. Sir John's successor was Sampson Wright who, as well as continuing the patrols, rebuilt his Office after it was damaged by fire during the Gordon Riots the same year.

These patrols of full time policemen were sometimes called 'thief catchers' or 'detectives' and by 1785 they had become known as the 'Bow Street Runners'. They are credited with being the prototype professional police force in Britain, although there were never more than eight of them. After the Gordon Riots in 1780 a 68-man part-time night patrol was established, and a uniformed day patrol was set up in 1807. By 1821 the Bow Street foot patrols numbered one hundred men. Incidentally, the City of London's Aldermen-Magistrates established the City's first full time day police force in 1784.

Horse patrols evolved in a similar way. Sir John Fielding started the first of these in 1763 with eight men, to police the turnpikes around London. Although they were most successful, the money available was insufficient to keep them going at that time. However, the Magistrates established a permanent horse patrol in 1783. Its well armed uniformed replacement set up by the Magistrate Sir Richard Ford in 1805 numbered fifty-two men and became (in 1836) the mounted branch of the Metropolitan Police, which continues to this day.

Bow Street Magistrates were pioneers of effective policing in another way. From 1762 onwards they took on the task of coordinating the work of the stipendiary magistrates in other parts of London, although their statutory powers to do this did not arrive for another thirty years. As part of this co-ordination, Sir John Fielding arranged to assemble and circulate to magistrates across the country details of stolen property, wanted criminals and deserters from the army or navy. This regular publication was called Weekly or Extraordinary Pursuit. It was renamed The Weekly Hue and Cry in 1786 and later became The Police Gazette, well before Scotland Yard took over its compilation and publication in 1883.

For ten years after Sir Robert Peel set up the Metropolitan Police in 1829 the independence of the Bow Street Magistrates, and even their little police forces, ran on. The new Metropolitan Police Force did not set up its headquarters in Bow Street but was based in a building near the Houses of Parliament whose rear entrance, used by constables, ran through Scotland Yard. No doubt its Commissioners were keen to take over Bow Street's policing activities and with this in mind they leased in 1832 two houses (Nos. 33 and 34) on the opposite side of the road from the Court to provide a divisional police station with charge room and offices, eighteen cells, and dormitories for 57 constables. We found no record of the tension between the two Forces living in the same street during the following seven years, but no doubt there was plenty.

The Police Act of 1839 ended this with the transfer of all the Magistrates' "police" to the Metropolitan Police Service. The Home Office took over the leases of No.4 and No 3. From then on the police in Bow Street were part of the Metropolitan Police Force.

In 1876 the Duke of Bedford agreed to a 99 year lease to the Crown of the land at Bow Street needed for the Courts and Police Station at an annual rent of £1100, provided that the tenant bought out the leaseholders of the houses on the site, and extinguished a right of way. A short Act of Parliament was needed to achieve this. In 1920 the Duke sold the freehold to the Crown for £25,000.

Having obtained the site, the existing houses were pulled down and excavations taken down to below basement level. In this 'hole' were built separate but similar new buildings for the police officers and the courts. The designs were by the Government Architect Sir John Taylor. The builders were George Smith and Co., starting in March 1879, and the cost was £27,980 financed by a 4% loan from the Treasury over 20 years.

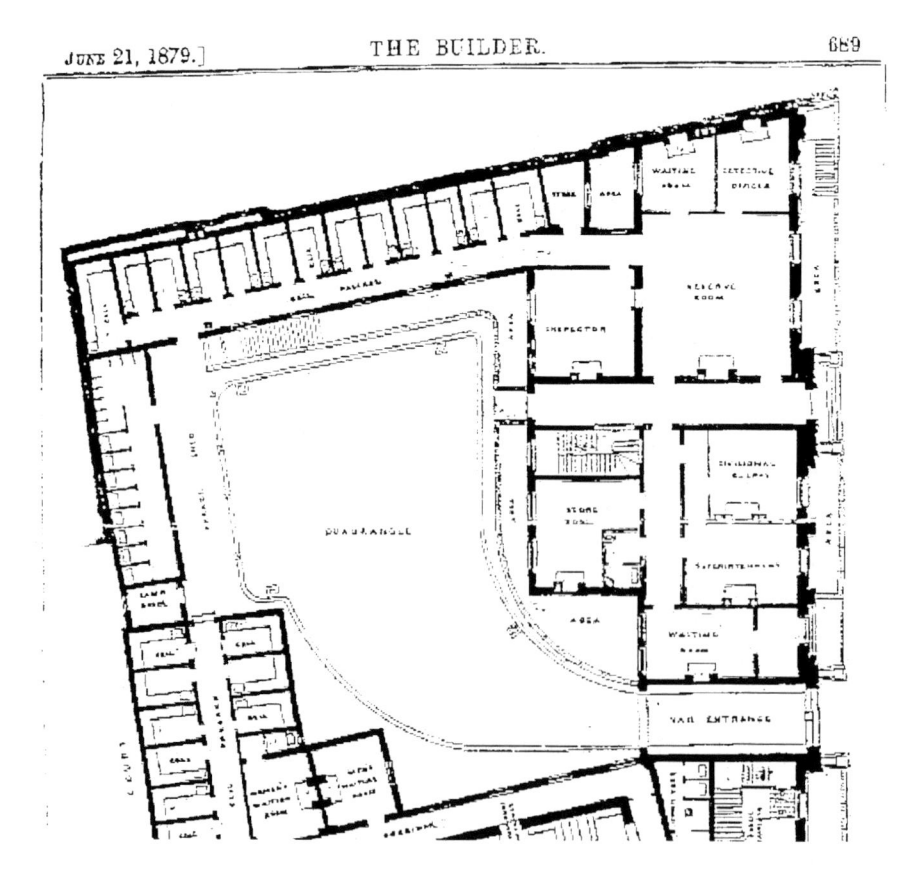

The original layout of the Police Station

An architectural writer of the time commented that "the disposition of the plan is not clearly expressed in the principal elevations. The architect was concerned that the Bow Street front of both buildings (which adjoin but do not connect) should be "of rather ornamental character, so as to harmonise to some extent with the opera house opposite." Three designs for the façade were prepared (which we have seen) showing that the façade style was not integral with the rest of the building but a separate decision. I found it amusing that when we wanted to change the interior but not the façade we were accused by planners of 'facadism'. That was exactly the concept for the original building we had to preserve!

Like its predecessor down the road, the Police Station was initially a section house more than it was an office. The three upper floors were used as large dormitories for 106 Police Officers. The kitchen and mess room were in the basement. Policing the Division was managed from the ground floor. I have reproduced only the ground floor plan and front elevation in this book but all the original plans and elevations are held in police records. At the rear there was at that time a parade shed backing on to Crown Court and a single storey line of 15 cells lean-to against buildings where the passage way known as Martlett Court now runs. There were not enough cells and in 1903 five new cells and a matron's room were built in place of the parade shed, at a cost of £4,200. (Bow Street was the first place where women were employed by the Metropolitan Police in 1890. (They were Civil Service matrons..)

The parade room, which lies under the yard, was probably built at the same time. In the main building, cubicles were fitted into the dormitories and a new bathroom was provided.

In 1906/7 the buildings that abutted the south side of the property were pulled down and Martlett Court was realigned alongside the cell block. This block gained an upper storey and a new outer wall. Further changes were made inside the building. The rebuilt cell block is shown in a picture in police archives of suffragettes holding a tea party in the service yard during their campaign for the women's vote. I cannot reproduce this picture but I can show a picture of the award winning policemen of about that time.

In 1915 the turmoil of world war required the construction of a temporary building above the yard to provide for the registration of aliens.

There was a battle here in 1919 in which 50 policemen held back a crowd of about 2,000 US, Canadian and Australian servicemen who attacked the Police Station. There were many injuries and arrests were made.

The next big change came in 1925 when the section house was closed and the basement of the Police Station was converted to provide the Aliens Registration Office with the entrance through a new door into Martlett Court. The first floor was turned over to offices. The alien registration building in the yard was pulled down. The door at the front used by the public and detectives was converted to be a window, possibly for increased security. A second new door in Martlett Court led to four sets of new senior officers' married quarters at the top of the building, although these were later displaced by offices.

Alien Registration was moved to another place in London in 1940 and offices spread into the basement. In later years the offices were altered and subdivided from time to time so that the interior now bears almost no resemblance to that originally built.

In contrast, the adjoining Magistrates Courts have been little changed, apart from the addition of an extra court and extension of the custody suite. The interior still has most of its original interior features.

In 1949 the Commissioner initiated a collection of Police memorabilia which was housed in Bow Street Police Station until 1967 and became known as the Historical Museum. There is now a society interested in police history, which is known as 'The Friends of the Historical Museum'.

The Police Station was replaced in 1993 by a new building on the south side of Covent Garden. The old building has been rotting away under the eyes of 24-hour security guards since then.

In 1995 the listed building was something of a liability, having a low leasehold value at that time (£2.2M) not least because of the difficulties and the costs of conversion to another acceptable use. Yet it was a fine Victorian Police Station that had to be preserved and could not be sold because that might imperil the security of the Magistrates Courts. With this in mind The Metropolitan Police chose the building for a national police museum because it stood in the street that was both the ancestral home of London and England's policing and was convenient for the tourist crowds in Covent Garden.

Five years later my consortium agreed to take on this responsibility and to maintain the long and fruitful police presence in Bow Street at current valuation and at negligible cost to the public purse. We also agreed to produce the museum the Police wanted. How we proposed to alter the building to museum use is described in Chapter 21.

Before we get to this I shall describe the museum itself. We had to write a description of our museum proposal for the planning application. This is reproduced in the next chapter. It is the only description ever published before this book was written. It appeared on the Web, in the newsletter called "The Runner" which we produced to tell people what was happening, and in a glossy brochure that went in with the planning application forms. Salmon Harvester also showed the brochure to potential tenants of the proposed offices. These were to occupy about half of the property and pay for everything we did.

12

The Museum Concept

The museum, which is the joint proposal of the City of London Police and the Metropolitan Police, is intended for visitors who may be Londoners or may be tourists.

It will give equal prominence to explaining modern policing, providing interactive experiences of police tasks, and displaying police memorabilia from the forces' large collections.

Once visitors go through the door they will cease to be just observing the police. Instead, they will be immersed in trying out policing tasks. Through this they should feel the emotions and social pressures which affect police officers, should see how technology is used to fight crime or maintain order, and should hear the true stories of past policing. The concept owes something to the success of interactive science centres but takes the approach into more emotional territory. This is far more fun than simply observing the police's museum exhibits and will minimise the obstruction to understanding that can arise from prejudices about the police.

The tone will be informative - and neutral with regard to contentious matters. However the designers feel that London's extraordinary success is rooted in the stability provided by sound policing, and this should be evident. Foreign tourists should have a rare insight into the culture and history of London and should leave with a good 'understanding of the advantages of the British approach to policing.

This kind of museum needs to be kept up to date and it will be designed in the form of a wide variety of "scenarios" each of which can be replaced at any time. Within each of these scenarios the visitors will be able to undertake tasks, either individually or collectively of the kind that an officer might meet on the beat. (See the illustrations)

The scenarios will come from various historic periods, and will feature all kinds of additional information. Their subject matter will be quite diverse and, for example, might include detecting burglary, crowd management, traffic control, major accident recovery, identifying suspects, counterfeiting, domestic incidents, using dogs to detect drugs and explosives, river policing, preventing shops or pubs giving short measure, mounted police and searching for fugitives. There will also be a courtroom for mock trials.

Emotions might be triggered by a visit to the old cells, and by a full presentation of the way in which all of the former Police Station was used at different times. The history of policing London and the story of Bow

Street itself as the historic location for police and magistrates will be told. Records and historic objects lent to the museum by the police will add to its interest and authenticity, and provide a deep resource of further information for those who are most interested.

The proposed title for the museum is THE BEAT, chosen to reflect the variety and uncertainty of normal police work.

MUSEUM ARRANGEMENT

Museum visitors will enter the building up the steps and through the Police Station door in Bow Street and an inner glass door. Pre-arranged school parties may be escorted in by way of the steps on the corner down into the area and through the basement door. Most of the visitors will leave through the second front door in order to minimise doorway congestion.

The ground floor of the old building to the left of the doorway will be the ticket office and shop. It will be opened up by partial removal of walls. Details of this are being discussed with English Heritage. Three large windows facing Bow Street and vaulted ceiling arches will add character.

There will be room to queue for admission within the shop and entry to the museum will be through the existing door at the rear of the old building into a central foyer with staircases plus lift for the disabled. Visitors will be free to descend to the spacious basement off which there will be three or four rooms for mock trials, viewing films and school parties. On the ground floor the cells will be preserved just as they are and there will be other exhibits. An upper ground floor in the new building will contain further exhibits.

The cells at the first floor level will be altered for use as museum operator facilities, storage and workshops.

The museum will be open seven days a week all year from 10 am. Closing time will vary between 6 pm and midnight. Except at high season the evening use will be for corporate functions, including service of food and drink, although there will be no kitchens on site.

The museum will become a major tourist attraction. It is being designed for a maximum visitor flow of 600 people per hour, that being as many as the space can comfortably handle. It is considered that there is no reliable way of forecasting the number of visitors who will come in a year. The normal method of comparing this with a similar place is not applicable because of the unique nature of the museum and its central location

The shop will become London's specialist centre for information about the police, including books, films, CD's, and slides as well as providing visitors with souvenirs and higher quality mementoes. Educational packs and an historical inquiry service will also be provided.

13

What shall we call it?

There were three problems about calling the place the "London Police Museum": the word "museum", the word "police" and the absence of anywhere like it from which an analogous name might be drawn and immediately understood.

The 'museum' word

Almost my first thought on seeing the advertisement was that for a large proportion of the adult population, and by extension their children or pupils, the word 'museum' means a stuffy Victorian building full of antiquities. Maybe they were taken to such places when they were at school and were disappointed to see only inanimate objects in glass cases, or old stones, with lots of long words and little current human interest. Maybe the people running the museum did not want you to upset their precious antiquities and secluded lives. Is 'museum' a title that will draw people?

The market research carried out for the Police before we came on the scene confirmed my concern. The researchers found that the public did not want it called a museum at all.

I had another concern. We were going to be in competition with a large number of museums in London. A few of these are very large and prestigious but most are quite small and receive fewer than 70,000 visitors a year. To be listed by the tourist industry in the list of London's museums would put us in competition with all of these small places Only tourists or Londoners with a specific interest in the police would be likely to choose us. That wasn't good enough.

One of the things that the tourist professionals observe is that in every major city there are a small number of places that the visiting tourist must see. Otherwise she or he will lose credibility when they return home and their acquaintances ask "Did you see…..?" My colleagues and I felt that we were not going to get on to the 'must see' list if we called our show the London Police Museum. Did we have to?

The legal documents which we signed with the Police defined the museum as:-

"An exhibition centre open to the public which will educate the public and young people in particular in an interesting and entertaining way about policing and other related service issues in society (but excluding for the avoidance of doubt the storage of archive material and antiquities except as agreed between the Landlord and the Tenant from time to time)."

This definition of our proposed museum is not the same as that used by the Museums & Galleries Commission which says that museums

"collect, document, preserve, exhibit and interpret material evidence and associated information for public benefit."

I am not sure that this comprehensiveness helps very much when ones primary aim is to attract and educate. It seems to by-pass consideration of how you define and achieve the public benefit, which is the main purpose. The consultant Bob Melling pointed out in November 1998 that

"There is a built-in tension between the perspective of the Commission and the aim of London Police Education, in which museum professionals could argue that the collection is not essential and is merely a tool of a pre-interpreted message." He went on "Is 'museum' definitely in the name? Is this the best reflection of the role, attractive to 'excluded' audiences etc.? Is it the best image to sell the entry charge? The police collection is clearly historically valuable and should be managed and made accessible appropriatly. To ease the ambiguity in role is there a case for separating the museum function in the organisational and financial structure?"

I looked the word up in a few dictionaries and found that in England "museum" is most widely used to mean:-

"a place for the storage and display of antiquities".

The Oxford English Dictionary was more helpful. It added a second definition.

"A building or apartment dedicated to the pursuit of
learning or the arts".

Our proposal would fall happily within this broader definition and hence it was correct for us to call our project a museum if we wanted to. Sometimes we did and sometimes we didn't.

For instance, to avoid any concern at the City Council and among the local residents about what we were proposing the planning application used the word "museum". It was for this reason that we used the word at the top of the description set out in the last chapter. This was not incorrect, but it would have been just as correct to call it an exhibition, or a visitor attraction.

The 'police' word

When I first discussed the project with the museum consultant Julian Ravest he immediately raised the same point about the word 'museum'. He said that the word "police" would also be off putting. On balance I think he is right. Many people do not like the police. As our work went on we found that a few of our potential consultants and many friends were very hostile to the London Police, perhaps more so than in other parts of Britain. People do not go to see organisations to which they are hostile. Maybe this word should also be avoided.

Whilst we were thinking about the word "police" we identified two other problems. The first was that the museum was not going to be about the police as an organisation. The subject matter was what the police do or did, which is called "policing". A further twist was that we found that not all policing is done by the police and what they do, and do not do, varies from one country to another and from time to time. Policing traffic is often a separate activity. In London it is not the police who seek out illegal immigrants, prevent smuggling, or protect people and property on railways.

An educational exhibition does not have to be complete but it ought to cover the main policing duties our society needs and not just those done by the particular Police Forces that were sponsoring us. So we agreed that it would be concerned with "policing".

Looking at the police

This helped with the second problem we had. This was that people hostile to the police might use the opportunity to get at them by wrecking the museum. No insurance company would cover us for this. "Vandals wreck the London Police Museum" would not be a good newspaper headline for us.

After a while we came up with a simple solution to this problem. Visitors would not be able to look at the police and what they were doing because they would become policemen or policewomen the moment they walked through the door. All the content would be presented to them as if they were serving officers on a visit for the day.

Finding a name

Before we were selected for the project I gently indicated the name problem to London Police Education and suggested that the museum should be called "Blue Lamps". My reasoning was that flashing blue lamps are the principal sign of the presence of the police on the streets now that whistles are seldom used. One of the policemen on the Board that heard this suggestion said that "Blue Lamps" sounded like a nightclub! Another pointed out that Bow Street police Station was unique in London for not having a blue light outside – at the request of Queen Victoria who associated the colour with her husband's deathbed. I needed to think again.

The name of a visitor attraction is normally used as a brand name. Almost every successful brand name has four syllables or fewer. A visitor attraction with a longer name will usually have a shortened name that is widely used. So we were looking for a name with not more than four syllables that was acceptable to the police and had a sensible connection with policing. Yet it must not contain either the word 'museum' or the word 'policing'. Lastly it must not be easily confused with any other place tourists might visit.

Dozens of names were put forward, some had strong advocates. One of these suggestions was "The Beat", although this did not meet with universal approval and we thought its excitement level was low.

What clinched our adoption of this name was our decision that visitors would become policemen for the day and the realisation that what they would then encounter in the museum were incidents as varied and as unpredictable as those which a police officer meets on the beat. Our visitors would have an experience akin to going out on the beat. The name very well fitted the style of exhibition for education and entertainment that we were creating.

Now we had to design a logo or trademark to suit this name. Sam Burford of Transient did this in dialogue with Will Baker, Alan Moss and myself. As you can see it hints at authority with its badge, at the uniformed service, at personal danger with its helmet, at detective work with its magnifying glass, and with the plodding nature of much police work with its footprints. Once it was registered with the Patent Office "The Beat" existed. We could roll out the brand.

THE BEAT

14

SMUCHII

You are standing beside a full-size, crashed car "set" on a motorway. Inside, a horrifically bloodstained driver manikin is badly injured but obviously still breathing. In the twisted rear of the wreck, two traumatised child figures are whimpering in shock.

High-speed traffic is flashing past, across a large video-projection screen behind the wreck. Another person (filmed against a black background) is projected onto screen superimposed in front of the traffic.

It is an elderly woman passenger, standing dazed and confused on the other side of the wreck, poised to stagger away into the passing traffic. In front of the wreck is a touch-screen, in standby mode. In large letters it says:

Respond to this incident? - Touch the screen.

Immediately on touching the screen the sound effects become louder and moments later a clock and a bullet-point menu appear.

What will you do first?
 Attend to the driver?
 Control the traffic?
 Reassure the children?
 Restrain the woman?
 Radio for assistance?

You touch the "Radio for assistance" option. Immediately the elderly woman walks away. There is a terrible squeal of tyres and a thud and she disappears.

The screen display changes.

What will you do now?
 Attend to the driver?
 Control the traffic?
 Reassure the children?
 Attend to the woman?

You have a hasty discussion with the friends standing beside you then touch the screen at "control the traffic".

The traffic flashing past across the background video-projection screen slows down and becomes quieter. The clock on the screen advances. The touch-screen changes - flashing an urgent message:

 "The old woman has died'.

One of the child figures starts to scream.

What will you do now?
> *Attend to the driver?*
> *Turn off the ignition key?*
> *Reassure the children?*
> *Attend to the woman?*

Unable to restrain herself, your friend reaches in front of you to touch the screen. She picks, "Reassure the children".

The clock on the screen advances a couple of minutes and the screaming subsides. The touch-screen flashes with another urgent message: "The driver has died of untreated blood-loss. Immediate first aid could have saved him."

Real smoke suddenly starts to billow up from the crumpled engine compartment. People in the slowly passing cars, seen on the large background screen, are reacting to the sight of the dead woman behind the wreck.

What will you do now?
> *Fetch a fire extinguisher from your patrol car?*
> *Turn off the ignition key?*
> *Get the children out of the car?*
> *Cover the body of the dead woman?*

You touch, "Fetch a fire extinguisher from your patrol car". The clock on the screen advances another minute. With a deep roar, the wrecked car is suddenly engulfed in flames, with bright, flickering red lights hidden inside it, and flames, smoke and cross fading spotlights are projected onto the gauze screen behind.

The touch-screen flashes:
> "You cannot save the children now!
> Why didn't you get them out of the car?"

Approaching police and ambulance sirens are heard.
> **Your "score" is displayed.**

Yes, this is the draft of the script for a type of interactive experience that we have called a SMUCHII. The name comes from the initial letters of the words I wrote down to describe what we were proposing: - Serial Multi-Choice Human Interest Interactive.

Three months after we were selected for the project I gave the name Hot Spots to places where two or more people can stand, as if they were policemen on the beat. On inserting a card into a control panel nearby an incident will appear in front of the person and he or she will have to decide what to do. The image will respond accordingly. The incident could be a traffic accident, encounter with a group of illegal immigrants, a rowdy crowd, a stolen vehicle, a domestic row, a siege, an attack on a VIP, a street fight, a fire and so on. The incident will be suited to the age and abilities of the pretend policeman (visitor) as revealed by the card inserted, but may be from a different historical period with background and sound effects which match.

The available reaction choices will be shown on the control panel, including drawing a truncheon, blowing a whistle, a mobile radio call, tear gas, dog, horse, vehicle or just making a quick exit. A policeman/woman whose face appears on screen can also be consulted. There is scope here either to show the danger of innocent misinterpretation of an apparent crime scene or the need for precise procedures. There will be a prompt to secure that the incident is reported in writing afterwards, possibly with competitive marking and prizes.

Alan Moss noted that the police schools involvement programme had the themes of personal safety, crime and its consequences, drugs, bullying and so on. He thought that some of these subjects would naturally lend themselves to inter-active escalating scenarios whereby the consequences of, say, not responding appropriately to verbal abuse can lead to worse behaviour.

The more advanced proposal for SMUCHII emerged from this initial thinking during a brainstorming session between Michael Hobson, Ian Russell, Nick Ferenczy and myself. We were trying to pin down the practicalities of a visitor playing a policeman and responding to a situation that was changing as he walked towards it. We needed to identify decision points and limit the options available. As we talked we became aware of the really difficult decisions that sometimes faced a policeman and the emotional consequences for him and others which could arise subsequently.

When later we discussed this with former police officers we found that most had faced dilemmas over instant decisions like those in the above example. No training could eliminate problems to which there might be no right answer – except with the benefit of hindsight. Training videos used at police colleges gave examples of real incidents, which we could work up.

Other scenarios no less challenging soon came to mind. There were opportunities for either individual, two-person or group decision-making. The acceptance of a group decision, such as could occur in a pub brawl, has extra dimensions. In every SMUCHII the visitor would not easily forget what he or she had seen or felt.

A simple set can be used for different video programmes. The programmes might be matched to the age and experience of visitors or to an historic period, or even show differences between day and night. The possibilities are not limited, but filming costs limit what is practical.

The key elements of the SMUCHII are the script, the permanent set (which may include real museum objects interesting in their own right), the 20-30 audio-video clips which will need co-ordination of projection on to wrap around screens, the instruction and response mechanism for the decision making, and the timings. In some SMUCHII visitors would fill a room, standing or seated. In other cases they would stand back as if in a control room for CCTV or a helicopter hovering above. Normally, one person would be the operator with family or friends watching. Or one could intervene using a linked control panel. This is not a solitary activity like operating a computer.

The best results would come if the operators had not seen what had happened before, but it might not be practical to achieve this. People could get hooked on finding what happened if the decisions were different. An individual visitor should, however, be limited to one or two "goes".

One issue that we did not settle was whether at the end of the SMUCHII program we should reveal the "right" solution – that is, what a well trained policeman would do. Personally, I was against this, partly because it might spoil the experience for others following on (the answer would be passed from mouth to mouth), and partly because it suggested that there was always a right solution – which may not be the case. There was also the danger that it would seem to pit the visitor against the police, which we wanted to avoid.

Most of the team who knew about the SMUCHII disagreed with me, and thought that knowing that the police knew the right way to handle the problem was an important message for The Beat to convey, reassuring to visitors and helpful to serving officers. No decision had been reached on this.

It is tempting to use the familiar push-button, touch-screen or joystick methods of conveying the visitor's decision but the subject matter opens up other options. Police often use radios or loudspeakers. They physically adopt positions or move about to indicate intentions especially if people may not be fluent in English. A whistle blast may be appropriate. Modern technology can detect these reactions but where the action is not likely to be automatic the task of quickly explaining to people what is expected of them may be challenging to the designers. We intended to experiment more on this.

Other details to be sorted out included language recognition, language options, hygiene if objects are touched, technical failure defaults, and intrusion of sound or light from other features. In some cases the visitor might see a set that comprises buildings that he or she could populate with people from different periods of his choice. Managing a crowd was not so different a task in Victorian times and the differences in officers' equipment might be interesting.

We asked Media Projects to produce a pilot SMUCHII so that we could decide upon the best interface control system, test visitors reactions, examine the balance between immersive experience and dwell time, test graphic interfaces, test whether an on-screen countdown helps the visitor, and test the technology.

We wanted it to be an immersive experience taking no more than three minutes where the visitor will take away an emotional memory akin to those of a police officer, in a realistic setting as opposed to that of an interactive game.

The secrets of success with the SMUCHII are the timing, and the transition from one sequence to another. The length of the audio-video clip, that must allow for both fast and slow decision makers, and what happens when it goes into default mode because the decision was not made in time. These will need to be worked out for each subject by trial and error at this stage in the development of the product. Ian Russell wrote a script for a SMUCHII showing a policeman investigating a house with an open door followed by progress from room to room in search of the explanation. This allowed much more flexibility of timing. The running times adopted would have affected the visitor turnover of The Beat and therefore its profitability at peak times.

The SMUCHII provides experiences that are emotional and not intellectual. Its appeal is therefore much wider than that of most interactives. Hope and fear, horror and joy, the choice between fight and flight, embarrassment when the wrong choice is made, the call for comfort or help, the psychology of group reaction, and even mass hysteria can all be written in to the scripts and scenes. We did not explore it, but it may be that the faces of those present could be pasted in to the video clips to add further spice.

It is this characteristic of the SMUCHII that convinced me that it would turn out to be the unique selling point for The Beat. It would have taken it far above the dumbed down theme park attraction which is often deplorable. An essential element of this would have been the authenticity of both the scene and the experience provided by the police approval. Without authenticity of this kind the SMUCHII is likely to be of little value.

For commercial reasons our plans for the SMUCHII have been kept very quiet, and the Police were not fully briefed. Even now I have hesitated before deciding to publish them, and the team intends to defend its intellectual property rights in the brief outline given here.

15

Choosing the team

The character and quality of The Beat would be decided by the designers and suppliers who created it. Not everyone can do everything equally well and so it would have been stupid to choose these people before we knew what we wanted designed and fitted out. So I resisted requests to name an eminent museum designer during the selection process.

What I did do at the beginning is to explore the project with three consultants with relevant experience and a good track record. The first of these was Julian Ravest, a former colleague who is a museum consultant with a particular knowledge of and interest in interactive science centres. In addition to helping us with initial thinking, Julian produced an Interpretative Plan which gave us the focus for post-selection discussions with Alan Moss for the Police, David Lang for Heritage Projects who were the intended operational managers, and my co-director Will Baker who was new to this sector of the leisure industry. The four of us comprised the design steering committee.

To proceed on the lines suggested we needed a researcher to assemble and digest much of the enormous amount of information that appeared to be available from the Police. Sharon Feldman was introduced to me as a freelance consultant in museum work and we asked her to take on this role. It soon turned out that this task was far less straightforward than is normal when designing a museum. After showing us this, Sharon decided to pursue her future elsewhere in the museum sector. I decided to delay collecting the information until we were clearer about how we were going to use it, and could decide whether we could reduce the size of the task by being selective.

A manager from a leading manufacturer of simulators that happened to have its office next to mine in Crawley had introduced Simon Harris to me as a first class designer of leisure simulators. Simon and I had worked well together on outline proposals for the Royal Marine Museum at Southsea that came to nothing and he was now growing his firm Metropolis AV+FX. He came in to our discussions as early as anyone, enthusiastic about the kind of interactive show that would attract people and offer learning experiences. He was always far more bullish than I about the number of visitors we could attract through this means.

Simon introduced us to Dan Lister and Erik Dinandt of Eigg, who well understood the business and were a great help in showing the police people what the museum would be like when we were being selected.

It was Julian Ravest who introduced me to Ian Russell, who designs science interactives and has a show called "exploding custard" which he presents to schools and other groups with great results. Ian provided us with a fascinating paper on the uses for interactives and the opportunities to include them in The Beat. He is a very creative and inventive person but no manager, so after we had explored several opportunities we decided that he should work closely with me in creating the SMUCHII explained in the previous chapter, and should advise and assist the designers of individual features. It helped that his brother was a policeman.

In addition to giving us plenty of creative ideas and practical knowledge, I have no doubt that Ian would have helped to avoid over-costly interactives that are not effective, which we see in many places nowadays, and to separate the wheat from the chaff in this business.

Nick Ferenczy, who is a long-time friend of Will Baker, writes scripts for children's books and shows. We thought that we would use this experience for some of our work even though we had decided not to use text to explain displayed material – on the grounds that it is seldom read. The proposed Virtual Museum can carry text and can easily offer this in different languages.

If a display cannot be understood with no more than a few words of text it has probably been wrongly designed or should not have been there in the first place. With many Londoners as well as tourists quite unfamiliar with the English language we started to plan multi-lingual displays until we discovered their high cost. The show would need to minimise the need for words.

Michael Hobson was introduced to me as an actor, director, and producer of CD-ROMs who was very interested in the police. His creativity and practicality impressed me and he brought focus to the SMUCHII idea when we were working out some features content. He would have worked on the SMUCHII.

Thomas Lisle, the principal of Interpretations, introduced himself at a trade show as a specialist in secure CD-ROMs and historic building walk-throughs. We commissioned him to try out a "who dun' it" sequential scenario on CD, and a demo CD for the virtual museum. This threw up some interesting challenges to our early assumptions about what could and could not be done with interactive technology in both The Beat and the Virtual Museum. We seemed not to have got our approach quite right. We were going to use Thomas' firm for the computer walk-through of the former Police Station, including showing its usage in different historic periods, which would have been fun.

Designers

When it came to designing the exhibition I decided not to put all of our eggs in one basket. We had already settled that the space would be occupied by a large number of separate features, comparable with the unrelated tasks or incidents that might be faced by a police officer in one day. There was no need to have them all designed by one team and to do so would give an unrealistic appearance of conformity.

Not having an overall designer proved to be controversial and was unacceptable to some people whom we approached. In reality the design of the whole must reflect the austere interiors of police stations, within which the focus is on people and not their surroundings or possessions. Of course some co-ordination of graphics, signage outside the features, colour and imagery would be needed and this was a task for a good graphic designer who could work in a team easily. I had long experience of graphic designers who work better when alone and find discussion of alternative approaches to presentation to be quite troublesome. So I was cautious in making an appointment.

My search was for someone with the required drive, good commercial experience, design flair, and the kind of personality that would work easily with our diverse and creative team without being swamped or sidelined. I chose Lance Bohl, who runs a small firm called Foundry Design, located in central London. He produced our newsletter "The Runner" in three editions, and helped with other tasks before the work was stopped.

We set a limit of six different designers for the features. Had any of our first choice disappointed us we would have found a substitute. The designers needed to be firms that were strong in different ways as our features varied in content and requirements. However, all six firms would have had to have research ability and a full understanding of designing exhibitions for which the public were paying.

One point that had come home strongly in our discussions is that the preparation of working drawings and specifications for everything that had to be done would be very expensive. Designers have a habit of changing their ideas as they go along, and the process must not inhibit this. If a new way of handling something came to the designer's mind when the feature was half-built, and it didn't add to costs, we wanted to be able to say yes without having to pay over the odds because it was a variation from the specification.

We were not going to seek very robust fit-outs but rather to accept short lives and replacement of many installations. Therefore we wanted the design and fit-out to be integrated as far as possible.

We looked at the work of a number of firms in an informal way and went to see their studios and executives to discuss our plans. Some firms we met were used to working with clients who did not have much mind of their own, such as charities or local authorities and we felt that these might upset the Police or Heritage Projects more than was wise. We doubted that some firms would keep costs down to budget or control fit-out timetables. Eventually the six firms we chose were: -

- Harris Blyth
- Judah Design
- Media Projects (no longer in business)
- Met Studios
- Mongrel Media
- Past Forward (sister firm of Heritage Projects)

Management

Several of these firms offered to provide us with project management services, but we thought that this was better kept separate. We had seen in the construction industry the benefits to the client of using independent project managers to control specifications, costs and programmes, the site itself and health and safety issues. Having checked out Advanced Thinking Systems and spoken at length with Mike Howie the managing director we gave that firm an initial contract to manage the design and fit-out process and they started work on this. Their involvement helped to clarify many implementation issues They produced the diagram opposite to show the formal relationship of everyone concerned.

Abacus was chosen as quantity surveyors and contract advisers in order to minimise risks.

We appointed John Stevenson of Stevenson Associates as inventory officer to help keep track of all memorabilia and other objects that we had on loan (or owned). In addition to those objects being provided by the police, we were receiving emails from all over the world some of which offered us objects which had been in family attics since their forbears had left the Police Force. No doubt such offers would have increased once our plans were known.

John Stevenson was also working on the business planning and financial controls, using his experience of administration within financial institutions. I had run in to him at a training day run for a Government department and found that we thought on similar lines.

When we came to the Virtual Museum we called upon the services a friend of my daughter, Alastair Dryburgh, who works as a financial management consultant.

Technical consultants

The team was not yet complete because there are considerable technical requirements. The Rolton Group are consulting engineers with whom Will Baker has worked, and they had helped us with studies of the premises before Salmon Harvester took over the client role for this and continued to use their services. It was logical for us to use them for air-conditioning, background, security and emergency lighting, alarms systems, telephones, and co-ordination of computer provision.

Promotional character design

When visiting a trade show my eye was caught by some extraordinary electronic "characters" of French design offered by a firm called Cyber-actors. Specially designed characters representing different levels of policeman could guide people around the show, or answer their questions, or be used in press and TV advertising. Disney provides a good example of such usage. After checking out the technical merit of Cyber-actors with Sam Burford who specialises in computer graphics, we met with Patrick Galiano to clarify what they could do for us.

The Police were going to be very sensitive at any use of fun characters in The Beat. So we were going to need very careful scripting and control of the body language of the characters to avoid problems. On the whole I thought that a lateral thinking French design team might make this easier to achieve. We decided that we would need four or five characters of similar appearance and prepared an initial brief for their design.

Researchers

It was probably going to be worthwhile to do market research with the prototype characters to see how well they would catch on with the public. For this we would have used Peke Research to brief and manage the field researchers provided by one of the big firms. The Director, Katherine Evans has been very astute and economical of resources when I have needed such work done before. Similar testing with the public might be needed with some of the features.

THE MISSING MUSEUM

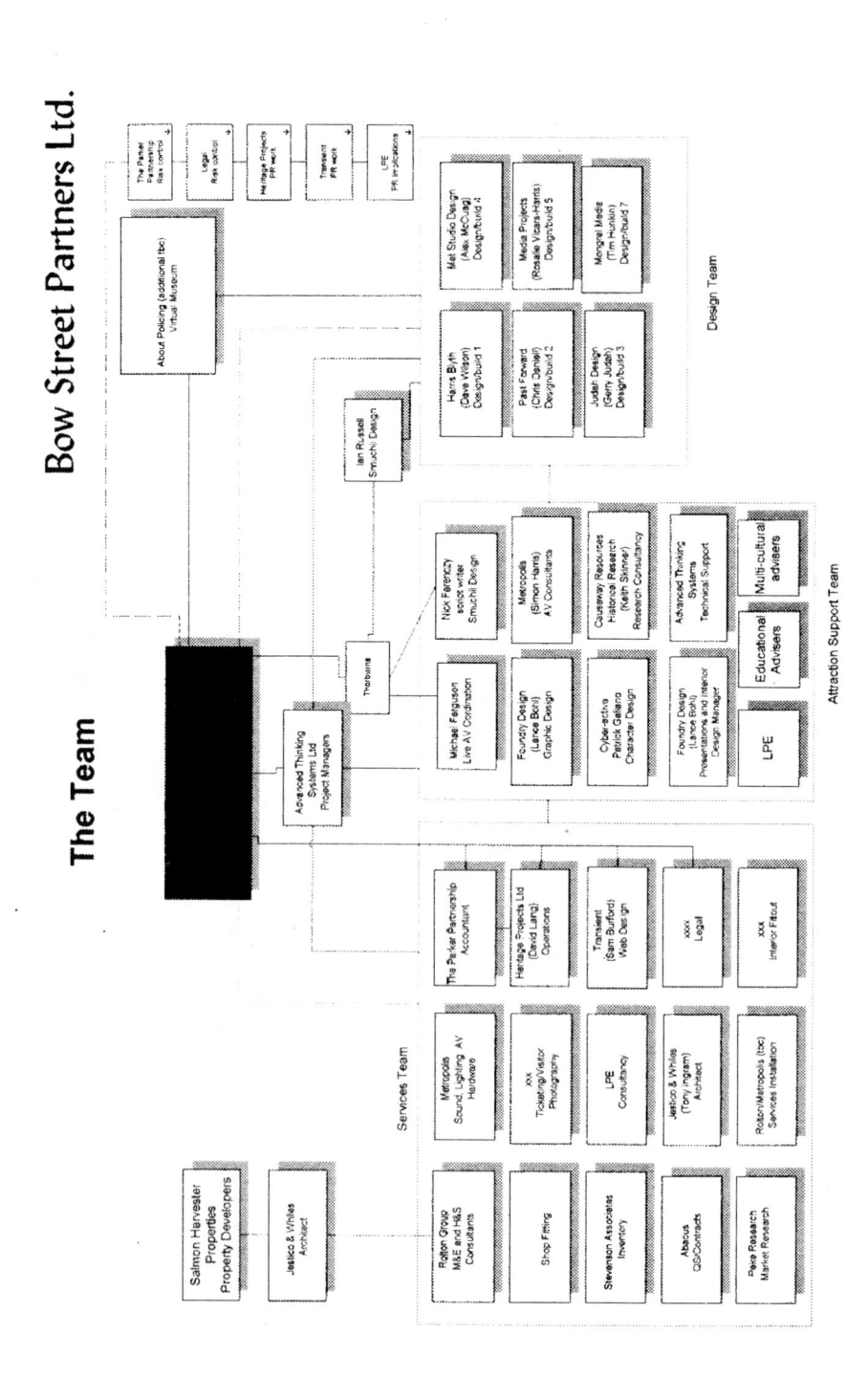

Bow Street Partners Ltd.

The Team

Design Team
- The Parker Partnership Risk control
- Legal Risk control
- Heritage Projects PR work
- Transient PR work
- LPE PR implications
- About Policing (additional tbc) Virtual Museum
- Mei Studio Design (Alec McCung) Design/build 4
- Media Projects (Rosalie Vicars-Harris) Design/build 5
- Mongrel Media (Tim Hunkin) Design/build 7
- Harris Blyth (Dave Wilson) Design/build 1
- Past Forward (Chris Daniel) Design/build 2
- Judah Design (Gerry Judah) Design/build 3
- Ian Russell Smurchi Design

Attraction Support Team
- Nick Ferenczy script writer Smurchi Design
- Metropolis (Simon Harris) AV Consultants
- Causeway Resources Historical Research (Keith Skinner) Research Consultancy
- Advanced Thinking Systems Technical Support
- Multi-cultural advisers
- Michael Ferguson Live AV Coordination
- Foundry Design (Lance Bohl) Graphic Design
- Cyber-active Patrick Gallena Character Design
- Foundry Design (Lance Bohl) Presentations and Interior Design Manager
- Educational Advisers
- LPE
- Thorburns
- Advanced Thinking Systems Ltd Project Managers

Services Team
- The Parker Partnership Accountant
- Heritage Projects Ltd (David Lang) Operations
- Transient (Sam Burford) Web Design
- xxx Legal
- xxx Interior Fitout
- Metropolis Sound, Lighting, AV Hardware
- xxx Ticketing/Visitor Photography
- LPE Consultancy
- Jestico & Whiles (Tony Ingram) Architect
- Rotor/Metropolis (tbc) Services Installation
- Salmon Harvester Properties Property Developers
- Jestico & Whiles Architect
- Rotor Group M&E and H&S Consultants
- Shop Fitting
- Stevenson Associates Inventory
- Abacus QS/Contracts
- Pera Research Market Research

Catherine Morris is a different kind of researcher. She is good at unstructured interviewing, and is not troubled if the situation she encounters is unpredicted. She interviewed the occupants of the flats overlooking the site to see what they felt about the proposed new building, and then began work on collecting information for the features on dogs and horses.

For research on the content of the features the researchers used by the design teams would have supplemented her services, and they would also guide us towards the best fit-out firms to use. They should also ensure that all policing methods shown were correct and all equipment or other articles were authentic or authentic replicas.

Bob Melling of Chromus is an IT systems consultant with a particular interest in museums. He helped to clarify the options in the earlier stages of our thinking, but I think that he was losing interest as the pieces fell in to place.

There is no doubt that the involvement of all these creative people would have generated its own dynamic. It could have taken us in to new realms of image and presentation. They and not the board of Bow Street Partners Ltd would have decided the nature of The Beat. There would have been mistakes and some features would not have lasted long. Any could be replaced. The process would have been cellular and organic and this would make the resulting exhibition stand out from its competitors.

16

Commissioning the design and fit-out

We planned to commission the detailed design work for the museum just as soon as the lease was signed, which would have been a few weeks after planning permission was issued. To prepare for this I drew out from our work what I thought was most useful to the design process. All the designers were going to be sent a guidance document, which we called "The Commissioning File" setting out our aspirations (seethe next chapter) and other advice, including a list of all the features we were proposing. The text is set out below.

Each design firm would be allocated some features to design. They would be provided with a brief and invited to come to a meeting with the project managers and myself at which we would answer questions and discuss practical matters such as contracts.

Before these meetings took place I intended to call a meeting of everyone involved to discuss more general matters, use of SMUCHII's and the contributions of Ian Russell, Lance Bohl and Simon Harris all of whom had responsibilities across the board. To start this meeting off I was proposing to make the following speech: -

"The author, J.G.Ballard has said many times that he sees a world of mind-numbing boredom, of total suburbanisation of the planet, interrupted by totally unpredicted acts of violence.

"I am the oldest person in the room and I can remember the last great violence - the Second World War. After this exciting and frightening event we reverted to the comfort convenience, endless tasks and boredom of suburban living.

"The curry powder which makes this suburban life bearable is a mixture of recreational sex, stardom, adventure holidays, and theme park escapism. But all the time we live in fear of personal or state violence.

"The only protection we have from this violence which haunts us is the police. So there is very great interest in what the police sees and does. It is probably the only subject for enjoyable theme park escapism that goes to the heart of society - all society.

"In our project we are not just creating another visitor attraction to pep up and while away a safe suburban day. We are giving our visitors a glimpse of just how they are protected from the violence that is a threat to our society. This makes our project different in kind from all the other visitor attractions and museums we know.

The nearest parallel is probably the great panoramas of battles that are pilgrimage sites in eastern Europe, which similarly deal with the violence that is the ultimate threat to our society..

"So you see that our attraction has to trigger human emotions, it has to touch on contentious issues, it has to handle violence and the threat of violence in an acceptable way, but should not itself act as a stimulus for violent thoughts and actions.

"Our unusual way of procuring the design - commissioning six design teams and further advisers - was chosen because of the difficulty and importance of doing these things. We shall all learn from one another as we go along, and when we open we shall have something that is really in a different league from what each of us has worked on before.

"As we work on the project we shall be meeting people who have their own ideas of what we should be doing, including but not exclusively the police officers and the teachers. I do not want to exclude their ideas but they may have to be adapted before they can be adopted. They do not understand the breadth of our purpose or the best use of media, and they do not control the purse strings. We shall be looking for the best proposals and trying to make them better within our view of what we are doing not theirs.

"When we started out on this project I had to pick a budget figure for the creation of the attraction. This has not changed but inflation and unexpected demands have taken their toll, so it now looks a bit tight. I am willing to increase the figure by attracting sponsors if we can do so, but not at the expense of editorial control. The sponsors may offer help in cash or in kind and I would like you to help in bringing them to the table.

"Mainly I am looking to you to keep us within budget by proposing designs which are not expensive to build. In my view the generosity of lottery funding has led the attraction industry in the direction of expensive whizz-bangs and high spec constructions that give poor value for money, like a Rolls Royce, but look prestigious to those commissioning them with other peoples money. This is not the direction for us. The police deal with people not prestige. Maybe THE BEAT can be seen as "dress down Friday" for the attraction industry.

"The person who is behind this project most committedly, and who has assiduously driven it forward through thick and thicker, is Alan Moss - a retired senior policeman who runs London Police Education Ltd. You will find him a help at all times and a wise counsellor.

"I asked Will Baker to help me with the project because of his enthusiasm and sense of fun and because of his engineers' understanding of bolting things together and reducing risk. He will help you to entertain and think laterally but in a practical way.

"Perhaps the most daunting aspect of this project is the variety and complexity of work undertaken by 28,000 police officers and their predecessors. Most exhibitions are intended to convey far simpler messages, using appropriate techniques. We do not have such an intention so this is not a conventional exhibition. It is to be a playground for learning about what the police do - and thereby understanding their role and how they can be helped on behalf of us all.

"Before we can design the playground we have to know more about what policemen do. After an unsuccessful attempt to research this for you we decided that it would be better for you and your researchers to find this out for yourselves. However, the division into features means that you will not need to cover the whole of policing. Of course, there is plenty of help available to you - just ask.

"Our detailed briefs for design work are part written and part oral. The written part is already with you and we shall be meeting you individually to back these up just as soon as you have had time to digest them and identify the matters you want to discuss. The process thereafter has been set out in the papers. Always keep in mind that after selection we shall be paying for you to deliver (within budget and timetable) the features you want to create. We are expecting you to take account of operator requirements and our overall layout decisions. Design co-ordination will be done with as light a touch as possible and will mainly concern technical and signage considerations."

The people listening to this speech would have received the commissioning file which read as follows: -

Contents

1. Introduction
2. The Features List
3. Aspirations [see the next chapter]
4. Movement and participation
5. Criteria for selection of features [not included in this book]
6. The team [see the diagram on page 94]

Introduction

This File has been prepared to guide those concerned with the design of THE BEAT.

It is confidential and its contents must not be divulged or discussed with anyone other than those named as its recipients. It win be updated from time to time. Specific briefs will be provided to individual designers and these may not be circulated.

No reference is made in this File to the marketing plan, the virtual museum, merchandising and retailing. All of these are the subject of separate consideration by the Company and its consultants and it is possible that some of the designers will be invited to help with these matters.

Purpose

THE BEAT has to fulfil both commercial and legal requirements. It must be profitable, and it must be an exhibition that will educate the public and young people in particular in an interesting and entertaining way about policing and other related serious issues in society. For the most part this education will comprise situations from which people can explore, and thus learn about policing. The presentation of information will not in itself be sufficiently educational, or attractive.

THE BEAT will generate retailing opportunities, and a centre for the sale of goods and services related to policing. There will be a small specialist shop integrated with arrangements for ordering goods and services from within the exhibition or over the Internet.

The sole client

Responsibility for THE BEAT rests solely with Bow Street Partners Ltd. The directors of this Company, Andrew Thorburn and Will Baker, will make all the decisions. They will normally do this after consulting with the proposed operating managers (Heritage Projects Ltd.), the project managers (Advanced Thinking Systems Ltd.), the body representing the Police Services (London Police Education Ltd.), and people sensitive to community concerns such as teachers, ethnic groups, nearby residents, community groups and local authorities. The designers are not expected to consult with any of these interests.

Quality

In order to achieve the highest quality the Company has decided that the design and construction work will be carried out by a number of firms each working on separate features. To simulate the reality of policing there will not be an overall style or mood, nor will the individual features be provided with a setting. It follows that there is no need for an overall design or master story line. But there will be consistency in the appearance of signs and print, and of quality, through the work of the Presentation Manager and Project Managers.

Content

The next section lists the proposed content of THE BEAT. Nearly all of the items will be interactive. A more detailed explanation of the purpose of each item on these lists and indicative budgets will be provided for designers by way of a brief. [These briefs are set out in Chapter 18] There are also some attractive sponsorship opportunities that will, if they are taken up, add to the budgets available and provide opportunities to expand the content.

Features lists

Key

* non-interactive
- contains SMUCHII
+ above standard size
> not good for sponsorship

List A -policing work

1. Officer on duty - uniforms and equipment *
2. Fair cop - procedures and practices of arrest
3. Officer placement -where the duty officer sends his constables
4. Benign policing - history of policing from Bow Street *
5. London's gain from stable policing *
6. History and use of Bow Street Police Station *
7. The cells +>
8. Court of justice +
9. Operation crowd management +
10. Looking for clues –
11. Analysing evidence -
12. Diamond bill +
13. Border guard -
14. On a high horse
15. Distinctive communities - the ethnic geography *
16. Flying fuzz - inside the police helicopter *
17. Lawful trade -
18. Help from dogs -

19. Traffic policing
20. Road patrol
21. Intelligence led policing *
22. On the river *
23. Police complaint *

List B - emotion generating experiences
24. Tracking identity -
25. Attending an accident -
26. Counterfeiting*
27. Dangerous work *
28. Encounters
    a. Open door –
    b. School playground trouble
    c. Chasing a fugitive
    d. Drug search
    e. Meeting unruly people in the street
    f. Domestic dispute
29. Conviction and sentencing>
30. 999 response-
31. CCTV chase-
32. Newcomers-
33. Fraud*
34. Pub disturbance-
35. Victorian policing-
36. Find the terrorists –
37. Press conference-
38. Stolen Property-
39. Planning a raid

Aspirations for The Beat

This section of the file is set out in the next chapter of this book.

Movement and participation

1. The design capacity that has been adopted for THE BEAT is 600 people per hour. For most of the time the actual flow of visitors will be lower than this.
2. The length of stay will not be controlled and is likely to be determined by visitor's off-site programmes of activities, especially bearing in mind that they will have to leave the building if they get hungry or thirsty. When it becomes crowded it may be unattractive to some people - who will then leave. For calculation purposes it is being

assumed that at full capacity the average length of stay will be about an hour. It will be longer when numbers are lower and for private parties in the evenings. This figure excludes people in the shop.

3. Thus the design has to provide space for this number of people to stand, sit or move about in reasonable comfort. In order to avoid congestion at particular spots and to allow people to spend as much or as little time as they wish visiting any one feature the movement of visitors will not be streamed. They can move in any direction they like as in a department store. The circulation space must allow for this to be possible at design capacity.

4. To maximise use of limited space it is envisaged that the movement areas, the passageways, will act as overflow waiting or watching areas for the interactives. However, adequate space for the normal level of observers should be provided out of the passageways.

5. Cross movement may slow down circulation and add to the total movement space required at nodal points. As a rule of thumb it is being assumed that every circulation passage will be traversed in both directions during a visit. That is, each passage will be designed for a flow of 600 an hour in each direction, and for people to slow down and stop when passing by something of interest to them.

6. It is expected that queues will form for the more popular interactives and space must be provided for these. In the light of experience some interactives may be duplicated to reduce queuing, e.g. the helicopter ride. Temporary exhibits in the initial design will be cleared away to provide such space when it is known what is most popular.

7. Full space planning and decisions on the location of particular features should follow the decision upon what features are wanted, with iteration as necessary.

8. Basic social research indicates that about 50% of the visitors will wish to try out the interactives and a similar number will be content to watch. These are unlikely to be in the same family group. That is, everyone in some group will want to have a go and for other families it will not be part of their culture to do so.

9. The aim is to ensure that those who wish to try the interactives have reasonable opportunity to do so at design capacity. The number of interactives that appeal to these people must be sufficient. Each of these people will, during a visit, spend some time circulating, or looking at things, or waiting their turn, so that only about one third of their time will be occupied with interactives. From this it has been decided that the total capacity of the interactives should be sufficient to occupy in an active capacity at least 100 people at any one time. If it is not possible to achieve this number due to limitations of space

and money it will be necessary to create arrangements to relieve queuing pressures.
10. People will become absorbed in the interactives and it is necessary in all cases to time the individual's turn and ensure that they move on and do not take a second turn. This can be done by use of bar codes on the entry tickets to trigger use of an interactive and prevent visitors taking a second go. The queuing arrangements need to provide for this.

A Constable at Bow Street

I first entered the door of Bow Street police station in 1968 as a fresh recruit from Hendon, with the number C 268 on my shoulder, and spent three happy and busy years at the station. In those days our shift pattern involved 4 weeks of night duty at a time, a very long stretch by modern standards, and the early and late turn officers were supplemented by teams of officers on "market" and "theatre" duties.

The biggest change to the area must be the removal of Covent Garden market. I am continually amazed by the transformation of the area, and the fact that the apparently permanent smell of old vegetables no longer seems to permeate the pavements. Bruce House in Kemble Street, a lodging house which accommodated many single men, often alcoholics, has now become a far more respectable building, and Middle Earth, a club in Covent Garden which attracted many heroin addicts, has long since closed its doors.

I imagine that the nuisances of rubbish, drunks and drug addicts still cause problems, but I am sure that they are not on the same scale now as when I wore my PC's uniform in the area.

Seeing the interior of Bow Street created a few echoes in my mind, but there have been so many changes to the interior in the past 35 years that I had to work hard to remember where the interior walls used to be in some parts of the building. The custody area of the courthouse next door has also changed substantially, but the features which have not changed are the stone frontage and the cells.

My first arrest was a man called Hugh Healey, a blind alcoholic who smashed a shop window in Little Newport Street with his white stick. I was a bit nervous at court next day, but by the time I had reached the witness box he had already pleaded Guilty and the Magistrate, who knew him very well indeed, said "Hugh Healey, you did this because I did not send you to prison yesterday, didn't you?".

And so he was sent to prison for 3 months or so because that was the only place where he was happy and secure. Very sad, but a reflection of the fact that Bow Street, like many other courts, did their best to deal with social problems by applying the criminal justice system.

If walls could tell tales, they would recount a lot of history at Bow Street, and I am really pleased to think that a museum at Bow Street would be able to reflect the building's tradition and heritage.

I am quite sure that the neighbours in Fletcher Buildings would not be happy to return to the days when stray dogs would howl in the night from the station yard (They sometimes had to "escape" from police custody to give everybody a break!), and do hope that the present proposals for the building can be developed so that everybody is pleased with the result.

Alan Moss

(who retired as a Chief Superintendent in 1997 and is now involved with co-ordinating the police aspects of the Bow Street museum project)

17

Aspirations

In the Commissioning File we said that all of the designers working on the project would need to be clear about what we are trying to achieve so that their work is correct in its focus. Our aspirations were as set out below.

High visitor numbers

Visitor numbers need to be maximised in order to achieve the greatest educational value for the police service, to support London's tourism, to pay the rent and cover the operational costs. It is prudent to assume that many of the people the police and our company wishes to attract normally find museums dull, are hostile to the police and think that entry money could be better spent elsewhere. These prejudices should be blown away.

This objective is best served by making THE BEAT appeal in one way or another to everyone from eight to eighty, and not just to selected target markets. In Chapter 8 the wide differences in the relevant characteristics of people, shown by social research, are used to identify types whose preferences need to be accommodated. Keeping an eye on what appeals to these customers, rather than what appeals to ourselves as providers, is the paramount design consideration. Pre-opening testing of ideas on members of the public would be useful.

Making THE BEAT a prestigious place to visit will help to attract visitors. Unique prestige can come by promoting it as the source location and only presentation of the London policing system. This system seeks to meet citizen need for law and order rather than protecting the state from the citizen. We hope to show that after the system was established it gave London the stability to succeed both economically and socially as the leading world city. Also, the system spread from London around the democratic world, and is therefore a part of the heritage of many other countries. This is a great story in itself.

Many of London's citizens and visitors come from countries where the police have protection of the state as their primary role, and in consequence show less care for individual people. It is likely that depicting this difference in a clear way will help people to understand much of what is contained in THE BEAT.

Warm welcome

The visitor welcome should be superb. There should be a sense of having arrived at a quality place that is not exclusive. Live colour screens at the entrance should show what is happening inside. Introductions should be easy to grasp. There should be no ticket barriers and no trace of officialdom or uniforms at the entrance.

Realism

The individual police officer or member of the public does not see London policing as a coherent whole and it would be unrealistic to convey it in this way at a popular exhibition.

Dividing it up into a large number of unrelated mini-exhibitions about activities which an officer might encounter on the beat is intended to introduce realism and to increase visitor capacity and enjoyment. The idea should be followed through in a way that ensures that this happens even though this conflicts with most exhibition design practice.

Unique emotional content

THE BEAT should mainly comprise things to do which cannot be done elsewhere. Sourcing information and playing games on computers can be done at home or school and there is no need to pay for space in central London for such purposes. Here we would rather enable people to try and carry out typical tasks of a policeman or policewoman and experience not just the intellectual challenges but also the emotions that would be experienced by the officer. Fear, anger, revenge, remorse, sympathy, hate, surprise, guilt, joy and so forth are all part of policing for both the police and the public. Most basic emotions last for less than a minute. Some are then remembered for a lifetime. This goes much further than providing experiences that have little or no participation. The designs should break new ground in this respect.

A great abundance of human interest can be added to this. So visitors should be able to see the emotions behind the official front.

Personalisation

We want to offer the kind of personalisation that is to be found on some websites rather than every visitor following the same route through the exhibits. This will improve visitor satisfaction, targeting, and sponsorship opportunities. It will provide packages for visitors with specific interests. It will allow them to choose between competitive scoring of results or non-competitive participation. Role-playing will be feasible. The way of achieving personalisation requires a separate design study.

Without judgements

It is most important that none of the treatment or content of THE BEAT should make a judgement on the Police Services, individual police officers, or the best way to carry out policing. Neither the designers nor the Company are competent to make such judgements, and to introduce them would undoubtedly stir hostility to THE BEAT itself among some visitors. Where an explanation of current police practice is needed or useful this should be presented without any indication or approval or criticism.

It is in order to avoid such judgements that the visitor will see everything from the police point of view but will not be given any training.

The aspiration to avoid making judgements on police practices does not affect the need for designers to obtain advice from a police officer upon proposals before these are finalised.

Discussion of issues and practices

THE BEAT will thus provide a neutral and unbiased arena for discussion of policing practice and related issues, starting from the human rights and community requirements of citizens. It should provide the facilities and structure for such discussions, one to one or in small or large groups. This will be of promotional value and will help to advance the interchange of views between police and public in a neutral place. Well-informed people and possibly the media need to be involved in arranging and participating in these discussions rather than the permanent staff.

Sound education

The content proposed is naturally educational because it enables people to learn about policing. The Police want this to be the centre for their schools involvement programmes.

It should additionally serve as a carrier for specific educational messages. Following consultation with the police these messages have been identified as follows : -
1. Communities cannot survive if they are not policed.
2. There are safe and unsafe ways of behaving.
3. The London police do not impose control over citizens, just obedience to the law.
4. Police have discretion about when to take action and have to exercise this without prejudice or corruption.
5. Action needs to fit the problem.
6. Most policing problems have been met before.

7. Restraining illegal action needs common sense, knowledge and experience.
8. Good communications within the Police Services are essential.
9. The police need to understand the views of other people in order to be fair and to achieve respect and support for upholding the law.
10. The police need information from the public about who is committing offences, where and when, and to be willing in providing eyewitness evidence.
11. Forensic science and technology improve effectiveness.
12. Police officers sometimes make mistakes.
13. Changes in police practice are usually triggered by "defining moments" after something has gone wrong. (It is widely believed that America has just experienced the mother of all defining moments in policing.)

The features are not to be designed simply to promote these messages. The messages should be slipped in consciously but not necessarily overtly whenever that is appropriate.

Selected memorabilia

Many people expect a museum to be full of antiquities, and some want this to be so because that is their interest. However, at the outset of the project it was decided not to create THE BEAT as a museum of the treasured possession, records and memories of the Police Services. Yet some visitors who have connections with the Police will be attracted by memorabilia and history. Some inclusion of these in the exhibition will add to the realism of looking at things from a police officer's point of view. We have the pick of the historical museum collection at Charlton. Memorabilia will also interest the curious, and the people who do not themselves want to participate in an interactive way.

Visitors should be able to explore the collections of memorabilia for inspiration, learning and enjoyment. It is this opportunity that makes the place into a museum. With it goes the obligation upon the management to safeguard and hold in trust these artefacts and specimens.

Exciting heritage

The Bow Street location and the building itself should be presented as a draw for those who are interested in history and the way people once lived. The cells can excite the imagination and should be a particular draw. Some people will support or sponsor the project if it fully and excitingly presents this heritage.

Humour

Our subject matter is rather serious and this will flow over into the exhibits if we do not include fun activities, cartoons and even levity. Difficult abstract concepts are usually best presented in an amusing way. We want to punch hard on this point.

Completeness

It is not possible to include all aspects of policing in the space currently available. What is to be included or excluded cannot be selected by a rational process without taking a point of view about policing which would be judgmental. The selection that is being made is based on quality of exhibit rather than subject matter. It could change as we advance.

Organic change

There will be a program of continual improvement. Also, the arrangement is being designed to facilitate the replacement of some features each year, or for some software to be rewritten and new stories introduced. There will never be an optimum design.

Quality

The best means of achieving high quality for THE BEAT is to give the designers maximum freedom, some competition and challenging approval processes. In the unlikely event that some work is not of high quality it will simply be replaced. The arrangements for this are being installed.

Appearance

The eyes of visitors should fall upon the interactives or exhibits themselves and not on the surroundings or signage. This implies a transparency in the presentation, which evokes the all-seeing eyes of good policing. Text messages are not wanted because they would not be read. Computer monitors are not wanted because they will harm the appearance and group use of THE BEAT. There is a utilitarian appearance to the interior of police stations and it would be appropriate to adopt the same style.

18
The design briefs for the features

Some readers may like to think out how they would tackle the design of each of the thirty nine features in accordance with the following briefs, which we would have issued to one or more of the selected design and implementation teams. They are unedited.

Other readers may not be interested in the details of content of the museum. They should skip to page 154 or thereabouts.

1   Officer on duty

Visitors will be able to see and touch uniforms, badges, warrant, waistcoat, helmet, truncheon, shield, high collar, whistle, torch, radio, notebook, advice manual, police car/bike, handcuffs, gas canister, sword etc. (see also Feature 43) Some visitors will be interested in how these accoutrements have changed over time, but this is not the main point.

The feature should show how the perception of a man or woman changes, in their own eyes and those of others including friends, after donning a uniform, and when holding a shield or canister, truncheon, torch or radio. Visitors will be issued with warrants for the day.

Educational purpose

The visitors will get to know about the basic practicalities of being a police officer, and how they have changed.

The feature will show how police communicate their presence to the public, and communicate with one another. They need to have an advantage over the public and be as personally safe as possible. Equipment improves with time.

To show the purpose and importance of the warrant.

Notes

Some specialist equipment is best placed with the appropriate feature – horse riders, dog handlers, detectives, etc.

There are old posters with derogatory words for police officers, from the Met collection.

Police wear badges for a reason, but a display of the badges and medals worn at different times by the two sponsoring forces is needed. This needs to link with features.

Simulated interaction between police and the public might help.

Lots and lots of memorabilia is there to choose from.

2 Fair cop - the principles and practices of arrest

We would like visitors to enjoy the challenge of making a successful arrest of a suspect, and to learn the rules. At one level the challenge is about securing physical ascendancy sufficient to restrain the suspect from escaping without using unnecessary force. Historical development of means to do this can be self-explanatory, together with some waving arms trying to avoid being handcuffed by the visitor! Means of calling for help and for transport to the cells are also important.

At another level the challenge is about only arresting a person who has probably committed a crime, AND who needs to be physically detained for some identifiable reason AND who has been selected after considering whether there is likely to be some evidence against him/her AND who has been given the proper caution. There are implicit or explicit sanctions against arbitrary arrest. This should lead to consideration of problem: -. such as racial stereotyping, "criminal looking" people, charmers and conmen (or little old ladies).

Put over the message that the values of the police are evidenced in their arrest practices but some mistakes occur which quickly lead to rancour.

Educational purpose
To show that arrests are not arbitrary in our system, and law, practice and limits to officer discretion closely regulate that police action.

Notes
Feeling the disapproval of the suspect and the approval of the public. Police officer reactions to people resisting arrests. Police officer fears of making a false arrest which lead to problems later.
The subject lends itself to a humorous approach.
It might include a robot resisting handcuffs.
Involvement of members of the public in scenarios.
Subtleties of dialogue and verbal protocol can be shown.
Show problems of arresting and cautioning person who does not understand London English.
There is opportunity for SMUCHII and other interactives and it needs to be decided which would be best.
Maybe a smaller scale SMUCHII—talking head or text only.
Show old handcuffs and other restraints.
History of revisions to wording of cautions.
Include Black Maria.

3 Officer placement

This would be an interactive which enables the visitor as Duty-Inspector to decide the placing of the shift of police men/women to match the requirements and priorities of the day. The visitor should see the consequences of not using officers effectively in terms of crime during the shift or longer term.

It would become self-evident that there are not enough policemen to do everything and that plodding around the streets is not often the best way to use them. This is a point upon which the police and public often disagree. Also, that policing often requires uniformed presence in numbers, and that has all kinds of consequences that might be simulated.

Educational purpose
The feature would demonstrate why officers do not pound the beat any more, and highlight the need for more resources and/or less bureaucracy. It would also demonstrate the variety of police work.

Notes
Show the frustration of the officer in charge at not having enough officers for all the tasks.
Stress of senior officers trying to cope.
Warm feeling towards collaborating police colleagues.
Maybe one could find an amusing way to show that the absence of the police presence can cause problems.
Possibly little figures of policemen to deploy physically.
Use a talking head – multi-lingual?
History of the beat patrol system.
Include the sounds of a police control room
Should be portrayed as a "try it and see" interactive.
Basic opportunity to reference lots of stories of police incidents.

4 Benign policing

The feature would cover the drama of a magistrate in Hogarthian London putting together a small professional force—the Bow Street Runners—reporting to him. Peel and Parliament defining the role of the citizen controlled police.
(Community policing as discussed earlier).
The absence of firearms.
The professional, not state or political, control of operations. The parts of the world to which these key ideas spread—and the contrast between London policing philosophy and the state controlled police services.

Educational purpose
To explain the role of the police in London.

> " The primary object of an efficient police is the prevention of crime: the next that of detection and punishment of offenders if a crime is committed. To these ends all the efforts of police must be directed. "The protection of life and property and the preservation of public tranquillity, and the absence of crime will alone prove whether those efforts have been successful and whether the objects for which the police were appointed have been attained". – Sir Reginald Mayne, joint first Commissioner of the Metropolitan Police, 1829

Notes
Distaste for those who see our police as there to protect the state and hence as a part of the present Government.
Possibly discussion between two people from different countries supported by dramatised details.
Mementoes of early policing.

5   London's gain from stable policing

This feature should be a celebration of success in policing London. Success should be measured against Sir Reginald Mayne's purpose – see previous feature – and the consequences of this for development, investment, safety of leading people, and variety of creative business or social life.

The method of conveying this to a multi-lingual audience will not be a simple display. The main features of the system used need to be identified (cross-referenced to Feature 4 – Benign policing) and each of them demonstrated, possibly interactively so as to show the alternatives that would be less good. The police's contribution to controversial changes in the law, e.g. capital punishment, confinement of suspected terrorists, gun control, can be shown by cartoons. So can the benefit/burden balance for the city.

Educational purpose
To demonstrate pride in the usefulness of the police's work.
To show the importance of good policing for London, Britain and the world.

Notes
Given the heaviness of the subject one might try to make many serious points in a humorous way
Maybe some shades of operetta
Selection of short video-clips to watch by button pressing.
Show police images intermixed with London images to strengthen association – but keep them up to date, not sentimental.
Show records of awards and success.

6 History and use of Bow Street Police Station

The premises were a home and an office for over one hundred men and should be depicted with utilitarian realism. It is not viable to restore as a museum piece the character and use of the interior and provide adequate public circulation to see this. So we need to show what the interior was like, and how it was used in earlier days, by creating an "electronic walk-through" of the building in use, maybe at both fifty and one hundred years ago. This involves recording the actual structure before it is altered and electronically superimposing suitable actors and props. Visitors to the museum would see this walkthrough and copies would be on sale.

A record should be added of the incidents which had occurred within and outside the building, such as the "Battle of Bow Street", the suffragettes tea party, and the appointment here of London's first women police officer.

Educational purpose

Exploring the building's use and history. Presenting the heritage that is particular to the location. Explaining how police stations are used. The presentation should enable discussion of why it is that we need so many more police offices and office workers now for the same number of residents or fewer in the same area of London.

Notes

Emotions might be stirred by showing the atmosphere of the building and pride in traditions there.

Visitors can go and look at some of the rooms afterwards, transferring the images on the video in their minds.

A walk-through rather than a fly-through VR method is preferred as this maintains realism and is not escapist. One might feature:

    a. *The first police office*
    b. *The first Met Police Station in Bow Street*
    c. *How the 1880 Bow Street Police Station was first used?*
    d. *The section house*
    e. *The aliens registration office*
    f. *1950's use*
    g. *1990's use*
    h. *Anecdotes of police officers who have served there.*

There might be scrolling interactive panoramas of the interiors. The scene in a room can come alive when a door in the panorama is opened. Objects can be displayed such as sergeant's desk, pictures of former use, typical furniture, names of the officers who have been in charge.

7 The cells

The cells are the most interesting feature of the building. Their condition is as it was when last used, or probably several decades earlier and they should be kept like that for realism. We want to offer experiences of being in a cell, seeing how they were used, seeing who has been held there, feeling the agonies of those detained—from the view point of the police of course. We want to show how it is essential to be able to quickly and easily detain people and bring them before a magistrate.

We have found that the original cells are of interest to those people whom we have taken to see them in their physical presence and they create emotions in some visitors through the primeval fears of incarceration and starvation. They generate feelings of empathy for those who have experienced them. They should not be portrayed as prisons, but places for cooling off, planning a defence, contemplating prison or worse, or avoiding a cold night in the street. There is lots of human interest here. Cells might be used for the following:

a. A tableau of a Victorian cell
b. A cell at night
c. Two cells for children to enter
d. An historical enquiry point
e. Policing advice point
f. An electronic screen walk-through of the building
g. Stores and duty manager's safe etc.
h. The viewpoint must be that of a police officer not a prisoner

Educational purpose

The educational value of a visit can be reinforced if their use in different is depicted and it is shown how difficult it would be to maintain law and order without the use of cells to hold violent or distraught people who are to be brought before a court. A cell is possibly the single most essential tool of a police force although it creates chores and the need for a court presence that may not be enjoyable for the police officer.

Notes

The gloomy nature of looking after prisoners is not a humorous subject— let us depict the sadness.. The public does not know the way cells are viewed by police officers themselves.

Depict the patterns of occupation at different times, and famous people. Memorabilia include straightjackets and other means of restraint.

Include list of famous people who have slept there. Do not redecorate.

Visitors will want to try out being in a cell—in quite large numbers

Provide photo opportunities, sound effects..

8   Court of justice

The context for this feature is that The Beat is not a show about justice being seen to be done. It is about policing being justly done and what happens when it is not.

We wish to feature firstly the proceedings in a court room and secondly the experiences of a police officer in court trying to show that he has obtained good evidence which is properly collected and presented and is without bias. For justice, how it was collected and analysed may be as important as its content. Yet those in the Court will put all kinds of pressures on him as he gives evidence including that from body language.

One alternative is to create a courtroom for this feature and be able to use it for other purposes. But there are other ways of staging the feature that might be easier to manage, less demanding of space or more effective.

Participation in the enactment of court scenes should be considered, assisted by auto prompts if necessary. The opportunity for a school class to act out a case with someone playing every role would appeal to many.

Experience of being in court would also be interesting to visitors.

Educational purpose

This is the feature that links policing activity to the enforcement of the criminal law, and the lawyers' activities in this respect.

It will also show the importance of procedures in securing justice and the key role that the police have in following and enforcing these.

Notes

There needs to be consideration of how party use interleaves with use by ordinary visitors.

Visitors should feel the stress of being in court.

Use voices and role-play to create humour, not jokes.

The courtroom will sometimes be used for other purposes such as discussions.

The portrayal of the battle between barristers in courtrooms or the feelings of the defendant, and sometimes the prosecutor are often portrayed with other media and it is doubtful if the extra dimension we can add would itself justify the space required.

A SMUCHII about cross-examination of a police witness is possible.

There is enormous scope for different SMUCHII to explore different cases generating different emotions.

The visitor whilst viewing a short incident might assemble the policeman's notebook on screen.

There may be some suitable courtroom objects to show.

9 Operation crowds

Visitors should see how the Police keep order within demonstrations, parades, football crowds, etc. Include how they exercise discretion in taking action, how restraining actions need common sense, knowledge and experience, and how there are safe and unsafe ways to behave.
Some understanding of the need to know and be alert to herd instincts among the crowds could be of interest.
The police have pointed out that they do not seek to "control" crowds.

Educational purpose
Indicating the moderating tactics used and the information requirements to isolate dedicated troublemakers.
Helping people to feel the great force of a determined crowd, and/or anger directed against the police force in itself or as proxy for unreachable authorities.
Showing the ways in which the public can help the police deal with the rowdy element.

Notes:

Somehow bring out the benefits of keeping the crowds in good humour through jokes or banter.
Create a typical control room, maybe a control room interactive
Show use of horses – link with Feature 14
Indicate human rights issues.
Indicate importance of freedom of speech and limits thereto.
Complement with press reports and pictures of demos.
Historic equipment for fighting demonstrations.
Shield
Water cannon
Bullet-proof vest.

10   Looking for clues

By trying out how to find various types of clues (some of which might be hidden in different parts of the building) the visitor would be challenged, and tested on his or her power of accurate observation. Tests could be set at different levels of difficulty. The feature should show the need for the public to offer clues and eyewitness accounts to police.
Activities might include
a.   Dusting for fingerprints
b.   Matching prints
c.   Scenario of a scene of crime with clues to find
d.   Notebook records.
e.   DNA and fibre tests
f.   Footprints and tyre marks
g.   Audio forensic clues
h.   Routines for remembering or clue finding
i.   Brass rubbing style clue records
j.   Sample magnification techniques
The relationship with the independent forensic science service and pathology service would be indicated.

Educational purpose
The feature would show modern, and earlier, practices in detective work. It would show the importance of forensic science. Showing how easily mistakes can be made. Show that every action leaves a trail.

Notes

Portray the thrill of capturing a key clue.
We could show how humour increases or decreases observational powers.
Maybe some humorous red-herrings.
A theatrical set behind a barrier.
Sensor triggered effects by touching certain objects
Scrolling panoramas where you click on clues—and try to get them all.
Fingerprint comparisons.
Essentially a looking and remembering interactive routine or routines
Forensic based interactives could be used.
Memorabilia shown might include lots of clues from past cases.

11. Analysing evidence

This will present the realities of putting the pieces of crimes together – and how officers have done this in the past. It will use an environment where evidence is not neat and tidily available. Probably set up an incident-room scenario.
The feature needs to focus on risks of false identification and/or prosecution arising from evidence being incomplete. It would include an interactive module giving visitors the opportunity to conduct an identity parade, and show other methods of person identification.
Catching and prosecuting lawbreakers involves several different activities, which are separately featured. This feature should link them. e.g. achieving arrest, finding clues, and giving evidence in court.

Educational purpose
This will show how an important and often tedious job is done.
The media often portrays analysis of evidence as no more than the lead detective having some kind of decisive moment when he alone sees what has happened, perhaps in contrast to Mr Plod. Normal practice is obviously not like that and this will be shown.

Notes

Convey something of the loathing, anger, fear and horror generated from real criminal actions.
Idiotic mistakes by criminals would be humorous
Real objects with stories behind them can be presented interestingly.
Interactives need to be invented. Might include a SMUCHII.
Eavesdropping on two invisible detectives discussing a case.
Graphic based Interactives.
Light boxes and electric button quizzes.
Original or replica evidence may be available for display

12   Diamond bill

[Listening to the news one lunch time we heard that some villains had been caught trying to escape with the diamond worth many millions of pounds that was purportedly on display at the Millennium Dome. John Stevenson and I talked this over during our pub lunch and decided to ask a photographer to go down there at once and film whatever he could see. I phoned Alan Moss and he phoned back later to say that as soon as the court case was over Scotland Yard would provide us with the story.

When the Dome closed down we acquired the display used for the diamond from its owner, De Beers, and the firm offered to sell us an imitation diamond for the display at a reasonable price. The Metropolitan Police can count this incident as a success. It had penetrated the gang, put its people into the Dome, and was ready to pick up the escaping villains before they could go very far. As a story it had what we needed.]

The actual showcase and actual replica diamond should be the centre of this feature. It is in our possession.

The object is to tell the story dramatically and ask searching questions, perhaps beforehand, such as: -

What would you have done if you had been guarding the diamonds when it actually happened?

Why protect diamonds.

Is this a priority for the police?

Could a private firm have done the work?

Did the insurers pay the police?

Educational purpose

To provide a case study of good policing with a subject of abiding interest in itself.

To show the use of infiltration of crime gangs, and covert operations.

Notes

Try to build the tensions experienced within the team as they wondered if the raiders would be caught, and the relief when they were.

Point up the nonsense of driving through the wall and not walking in the door.

Use original display and reproduce action and dilemmas of the officers handling it. Police films and pictures. Our pictures.

Newsreel clips.

Comparison with other cases.

Maybe a "How would you have stopped the gang" – SMUCHII

13   Smuggling

The goods or persons smuggled in or out of London by sea or air have changed but the process of preventing this illegal activity has lasting characteristics, and much drama, which are the fundamentals of this feature.

The damage done by smuggled goods, such as drugs, would need to be shown in order that visitors do not take the side of the smugglers. The necessity of preventing smuggling in order to maintain the fiscal regime may not be so well received.

An interactive showing the visitor acting as customs officer—maintaining great secrecy – and then the pounce would be attractive. This might be a SMUCHII although multiple choice is not a large part of the work.

Include smuggling through ports and airports of people (in and out), tobacco, liquor, jewels, armaments (in and out), controlled foodstuffs, and animals. Point up reasons and practices of border controls.

Educational purpose

This would show the importance and limits of an important part of policing London.

Notes

Pride in success or misery in failure to maintain good order in a field where officer discretion is minimal.
From past cases there may be humour that can be written in to the script.
Collection of historic posters to be displayed.
Memorabilia will need to be sourced.

[It is understood that catching smugglers has never been a police function, although the police may help customs officers where necessary. The case for excluding the feature in favour of one or more that is of direct concern to the two Police Forces may require consideration]

14   Mounted policing

There will be some horse-loving visitors but the main interest in this feature should come from people who are interested in how the animals are used for police work. An interactive that provides visitors with a brief time on a simulated horse doing a policing job is expected to pull the crowds. Other interactives may be possible.

This should be backed by the whole story of selection training and use of horses over the last century and more. Both Police Services must be included. The quality of the mounted police and the benefits from using police horses for different purposes. Should show uses for horses past and present and value of the horse. Also show human/horse interactions.

Educational purpose

This will demonstrate the work of mounted police at present and in the past.

Notes

The feeling of power which comes from the high position and the emotions generated by the presence of the crowd around them should be featured.
Also the horse-lovers feelings.
Cartoons and incidents please.
Possibly use slightly moving horses back and legs and head with large screen surround to provide a mount for visitors that gives realism to this work. Also sound surround with shouts.
Include training of horses
Selection of horses and riders
Change from routine to emergency activities.
Horse equipment
Riding equipment
History of use of horses.

15 Distinctive cultural communities

Firstly, we need to show the number and size of communities within London that are not culturally or ethnically English in character. We should explain that some of the inhabitants of these want to retain the separateness of their culture and others want or expect to merge with the predominant English cultural community, and so lose their separate identity. This information should be shown dynamically as the numbers and locations change over time, and go back a very long way. It is not a modern phenomenon. The outward migrant flows are also relevant.

Then we want to show the practical consequences for policing of these cultural differences, particularly the problems of communicating and understanding between the people and the police officers who do not share either language or culture. This should be very graphic and draw out the emotional frustration as well as the misunderstandings that are often met. The over zealous stop-and-search actions which so upset the middle-class black residents are part of this.

Educational purpose

Helping visitors to learn that differences in skin colour and behaviour are a characteristic of London and do not detract from law and order if properly understood.

Notes

Possibly a SMUCHII in which visitors have to act as policemen talking with other ethnic groups.
Minimise text. If used make it multi-lingual.
We must be wary of generating any emotion other than curiosity.
If possible use humour to demonstrate misunderstandings and avoid rancour.
A large table or wall showing on a large scale map the location and size of each community possibly with changes shown since 1800
Cartoon of London inflow and outflow of migrants
Snatches of languages used in London.
Hear the same word in a variety of different languages or accents.
Prints of migrants.
Typical forms once used by the Aliens Registration Office at Bow Street.

16   Flying Fuzz

This allows visitors to experience the inside of a police helicopter as in an operation or in alternative operations which require quick response or a bird's eye view. Very few people have ever ridden in a helicopter and this will be so popular that we expect to have to duplicate it. The outside of the helicopter need not be visible except for the doorway. Noise should be inside only.

Educational purpose

- To show that airborne presence and rapid response is selectively as useful to the police as deterrent convictions. To show that the noise of a helicopter which may disturb residents for hours is necessary.
Showing the proper use of radio and of safe flight routines.

Notes

The thrill of riding in a helicopter will reinforce the thrill of the action to make this memorable.
There could also be some interest in the panorama of London as a whole.
The interior should best be an exact replica.
Voice of police radio.
Possibly co-pilot's commentary.
In flight check by visitor.
This may or may not be interactive.
Speeding up and slowing down rotor
Tilting scene to show cornering.
Flying memorabilia to interest those who are queuing.

17 Short measure and diluted goods

This should be a light hearted and amusing feature. Visitors should be told that responsibility for this policing activity lies with the local authorities, no longer with the police, but sometimes the police may help, e.g. with vehicle weighing or closing down premises. A cartoon style explanation to be given of how policing of trading is needed to protect the consumer.
The feature might cover dilution of beer, cider, milk, petrol, cocaine, flour and short measure of food, liquids, coal and building materials.
Few people have observed the use of certified standard weights and measures and this should be shown. Also vehicle weighing etc.:

Educational purpose
To show that some vital policing is not done by the police but extends into society far beyond the police officers actions. Shows the need for constant vigilance.
To demonstrate certain dilemmas – such as the difficulty of preventing the dilution of illegal substances versus the dangers of making them legal.

Notes
The anger of seeing people being "ripped off" should emerge from the feature as well as concern about harm from substances.
Records of successful prosecutions.
Typical measurement methods – early and modern.
Many opportunities for interactives.
Historic measuring devices may be available for display.

18. Help from dogs

This should show why and how dogs are used, bred and trained for police work, their control, relationship with their handling officers and eventual retirement.
It will especially attract dog-lovers and the presentation should satisfy them whilst focussing upon their role in policing.

Educational purpose
To show that dogs are indispensable for some tasks, and how members of the public can help, and not hinder them.
To show their limitations.
To show the care with which they are used.

Notes
What it feels like to send a much-loved dog into a dangerous situation. And the satisfaction of success.
Humorous incidents should be selected
Cases from both Police Forces
Early types of dog used
Merits of the two or three breeds now used
Scene of use to search within a building
List of gallant police dogs
Human interest stories involving dogs
SMUCHII seen from a dogs view would be fun
Dog equipment on display – old and modern

19   Traffic policing

The feature should enable people to emulate police operation of the systems which have been invented to maintain orderly road movement and prevent obstruction –such as laws, lights, signage, markings, cameras, roundabouts, restrictions, police cars and so forth.

Educational purpose
To help the public to behave more safely and considerately.
To show why we are so regulated, and so penalised for disobeying regulations or orders.
To help children understand road dangers and road congestion causes.
To show how the police need to understand the views of people and exercise discretion.
To show the essential nature of road rules,

Notes

Demonstrate the frustration felt by the police when their controls are ignored.
Lots of cartoons—e.g. Giles
Roadside check scene
Horse vehicles in 19thC traffic.
Possible interactives of Point Duty, car chase, speed cops stopping vehicles!
A good computer game project
There is lots of memorabilia including Belisha beacons, signs, and pictures of earlier traffic including horse drawn vehicles.
Explain why, in London, the traffic police are not a separate force but the public transport police are.

20 Road patrol

This is about driving in London as viewed by a police officer. It should provide interactive experience of police driving including the routines when they call out a continuous stream of observations about driving as they proceed down the road.

Educational purpose

To heighten awareness of driving dangers and the ways in which they are tackled.
To provide understanding of the tasks of traffic cops.

Notes

Bring out the exasperation of having to deal with crashes due to drink, drugs, speeding, tiredness or selfish driving etc.
Should include humorous incidents observed. (Is it too saucy to feature a girls skirt suddenly blowing up to show her knickers? The reaction of the driver when it happened amused my friend.)
Police car interior should be shown
Visitors might sit in a simulated car and call the route as the police do.
Maybe a real police car on a simulator deck.
Maybe a tape is made of what the visitor said.
Old police cars, equipment and pictures should be on display.

21 Intelligence-led policing

This is to show the way that intelligence–led policing is practised now, and in the past, and to give an indication of its costs and any procedures involving the public. It will almost certainly have to be interactive to be effective. A scriptwriter from The Bill or a similar programme would provide a start but we need to focus on the operations and not the story. We cannot leave out such an important part of modern policing, and the way in which it complements other police activities, and have to draw out the innate love-hate human interest in conspiracy to attract attention to the feature.

Educational purpose
To show the value of using intelligence systems to foil crimes by gangs and conspirators.
To show the importance of discrete public assistance with this work, and the problems of monitoring this including risks to those involved.
To compare the effectiveness of intelligence-led policing with that depending upon overt presence on the beat, on call or elsewhere.

Notes

We are currently uncertain about what emotions the police officer feels when handling such matters and this needs to be researched.
Include policing of the Internet, and the dangers of costly mistakes in this and other fields.
Money theft, guns and drugs might comprise objectives of criminal activities.
Criminal activity may be explained with actor replication.
Perhaps SMUCHII style conversations and their consequences.
Memorabilia from major crimes—and stories of catching gangs.
City of London Police may offer good cases.

22   River police

The river police started to protect cargoes and lives on board ships within London before the Metropolitan Police was set up. They are now constituted as Thames Division of the Metropolitan Police with duties on water (including search and rescue in water which is not part of the Thames) similar to those of their colleagues on land.

This feature should show their equipment, rapid response arrangements, how officers are recruited or assigned to the Division, and the special characteristics of their role. And, of course, their history.

Educational purpose

To inform visitors about an interesting type of policing

Notes

Pictorial Humour around boats.
Design suggestions
Boats used now and earlier
Patrol routines
River map with historical references
Anecdotes
Use of divers
Interactives might include
Health check
Boat safety checks
Simulation of night patrol
Put video cameras in the boats linked to display screens.
Because the Division has its own private museum at Wapping memorabilia used for this feature may need to be replicas, unless surplus to needs.

23   Police complaint

This should present the full story of what happens when someone is unhappy about the police. It should offer the visitor the opportunity to investigate a complaint against a fellow officer. To offset the seriousness of the subject matter there needs to be some humour in the presentation.

If possible, the approach should be one that discourages people from complaining whilst showing them what to do if they need to.

Probably it will best be presented as a drama going through the different stages of the complaint with a real example. One should not assume that the complaint system always works as intended.

Educational purpose

To show that the police have to justify their actions to the public, not just the Courts.
To enable visitors to know what will happen if they complain and to have confidence in the system.
To show that the police normally but not infallibly respond to criticism in appropriate ways.

Notes

Show the anger of the police officer exposed to an unjust complaint, either himself or his colleague.
Action following a genuine mistake should be conveyed.
Access should be given to famous cases of complaint

24. Tracking identity

The aim of this feature is to enable visitors to discover the methods and tricks of remembering people and of jogging the memories of others. It should include the use of deliberate disguises and their limitations, forensic means of finding the right person and ways of tracing wanted persons. These matters should be experienced by the visitor rather than being demonstrated, so that the full impact of mistakes and successes can be felt.

The dangers of stereotyping should be shown. Information and pictures of currently wanted persons should be displayed and the public asked to cooperate in finding them.

Educational purpose

Show the risk and consequences of error in identification and the challenge of correctly finding people.

Notes

SMUCHII potential
There are believed to be interesting memorabilia that can be included in the feature.
Design suggestions
1. *Identity parade.*
2. *Identikit.*
3. *Head measurements.*
4. *Finger print records.*
5. *Electronic eyeballing*
6. *Show how people who are static can look the same. e.g. with actors.*
7. *Show how some people have problems in distinguishing between people of certain ethnic types etc.*
8. *Voice recognition might feature computer's ability to distinguish between true voices and top level impressionists.*
9. *Watching video clips, then answering multiple choice questions*
10. *Assessment of likelihood of guilt from appearance.*

25   Attending a road accident

A SMUCHII – which will provide an opportunity to experience the reality, for the police officer first on the scene of handling a tragedy alone, with the need to act effectively to minimise further loss. (See chapter 14)

Educational purpose

To show safe ways of working and the importance of good communications.
To show that police officers can make mistakes.
To show the importance of training and efficient execution – amidst emotional people.

Notes
Humour is not appropriate
 Crashed car with sound effects and passing traffic might be included.
Show road accident statistics.
Include emergency rescue kit.
Accident signs.
Means of preventing public upset
No warning before entry to achieve maximum impact.

26   Counterfeit goods

The feature should enable visitors to try police methods for finding out what is real or a fake in art, coins, Notes, signatures, and other valuable. Also show how counterfeiters are brought to trial.

Educational purpose

Show how restraining illegal action needs knowledge, how forensic science is used, that Police must not be corrupt, that police need informers and enforce law. Deter fencing and sale of designer fakes.

Notes

A popular rather than a property owners view must be taken in the presentation or it will not have wide appeal.
Past counterfeiting success and failures may help.
Infamous forgers detection successes.
Interactives can be designed around finding the fake.
Interactive examination of counterfeit Notes.
Specimens of counterfeit goods can be shown.

27 Dangerous work

The feature should show the nature of the dangers faced by policemen and the use of shields, body armour, dogs, radios etc. to protect them. Given that they are the cause of much danger, this is the only place in the museum where the use of guns will be mentioned. We want to tell of the gallantry of individual police officers, of awards for gallantry. Some aspects of this could be interactive and some dramatised. What does it feel like to be in danger? What is it like to receive recognition for gallantry? What training is there for the responsibility for pulling the trigger?

Educational purpose

Shows that police work can be dangerous. The overall intention is to make the public aware of the risk management now carried out by the police. And to make them proud of those who have taken risks.

Notes

Humour should be avoided out of respect for the injured and dead gallant officers.
We must also feature the Battle of Bow Street—where the Police Station was defended successfully in a street battle.
This is an area where there have been considerable advances in procedure and equipment during the last century that can be explained.
Might include also: -
Stories of brave policemen.
Bravery medals
Citations

28 Encounters

There would be four or five features under this heading. The intention is to feature the experiences of being a police officer through providing a screen-based SMUCHII. Starting with four similar features the encounters would be replicated as necessary to meet demand.

The visitor's choice of SMUCHII would be run by a single individual using projection on to white walls all the action being on video. New SMUCHII can be introduced or existing ones can be duplicated to meet demand. Each will need visitor controls, watching space and projection facilities, plus a scoring system as an option.

Educational purpose

The SMUCHII will entertain. Their educational value will lie in the way that they tell people what the police have to do and provide a realistic experience of doing it.

Notes

Subject matters for SMUCHII include: -
- *Response to suspicious circumstance—the open door—the policeman has been asked to investigate a house where a neighbour reports that the door has been standing open all night. A simple SMUCHII could provide interactive experience of the police emotions in handling this. A message is that some situations are best handled by the police not a member of the public because of their danger, the intrusion into private property, and the need to protect evidence.*
- *Disturbance in a school playground.*
- *Drug search to include a dog's eye view of the action.*
- *Chasing a fugitive.*
- *Encountering a crowd on rounding a corner.*
- *A domestic dispute.*

29   Conviction and sentencing

The feature should provide the thrill and apprehension of having the power to decide the type and length of punishment (historically including misery and death) for someone whom the jury found guilty. The need for punishment to fit the crime—whatever that means!
It should show that sentencing predate police forces. Sentences deter, punish and prevent. Once they also populated colonies for the benefit of their landowners and national ambitions. They vary in duration and type and change over time. They affect people other than the felon, especially families, gaolers, prisoner escorts, prison visitors, victims and witnesses.
They are decided by courts, but used by the police to warn and threaten. Getting these right is a measure of good policing, but sentences are never nice for the recipient. Also show the dangers of the power to determine sentences corrupting judges.
Educational purpose
Visitors would learn how sentences are determined and what options the judge has.

Notes
Use voting technology to gather views on modern sentences from the public—an interesting novelty given that no forum for this now exists.
Mention logistical problems when cells/transport ships are in short supply.
Gallows Humour might get a mention.
It is the judge who has the choice—within limits and conventions—so we could turn the visitor into the judge deciding what sentence to impose and why. Possibly use illusion technology to transform visitor into a judge. Or the visitor could be a policeman asked to suggest to prosecuting counsel what sentence to ask for. Or maybe one could tell the detainee in a cell the options for his/her future. Either way the normal consequences of the sentence need to be portrayed. We should not go back to medieval torture. Maybe it can relate to history of convict colonies.
The depiction of punishments like deportation, hard labour and hanging provide ready dramas that can be used to illustrate the dilemmas of the courts in imposing sentences of every kind.
Maybe an interactive element can provide a strong emotional experience.
Include last letter from the convicted.
Show use of ball and chain.
Replicas of items in the Black Museum, e.g. gallows and rope.
Community service order.

30   999 response

The experience of actually receiving emergency calls and quickly initiating the appropriate response. What does the call centre look like? What are the calls for help like? What does it feel like to choose the appropriate action? Who makes the choices? What happens when things go wrong? How are communication systems used?

This should be a simulated real time experience wherein responsiveness matters. Error feedback is essential. Maybe it could be a SMUCHII with the public seeing the video clips of consequences, not the operators.

Educational purpose

To show that whilst the calls themselves are sometimes of dramatic character the room receiving them is a significant resource whose use requires the making of many quick choices in real time. Also to deter people from making unnecessary calls or wasting police time.

Notes

Some calls or their consequences are undoubtedly humorous and a careful and tactful choice of these should be possible.
Show copy of a control centre.
Old telephones and radios as memorabilia perhaps.
Equipment for raising the alert, such as flashing lights, whistles.

31 CCTV chase

There might be several replicas of this to meet expected high demand.
This is a very simple interactive feature wherein one visitor in a control room follows an escaping shoplifter/vandal on a chain of CCTV cameras and targets a colleague by radio to apprehend the felon, who may get away.

Educational purpose

Shows the use of CCTV to deter minor crime.
Shows difficulties of using it as evidence in major crime.

Notes

Set of CCTV screens in control room
Possible live links to cameras in Bow Street.
Early TV cameras used for CCTV might be shown on the set.

32 Immigration decisions

The feature should enable the visitor to become the immigration officer handling various cases that raise questions about community attitudes and national policies. The dramas of such work should be incorporated. A brief outline of existing policies in words or diagrams anyone can understand will be required – this may generate controversy, which is good publicity on opening.

Assistance from an immigration officer is available.

Educational purpose

Showing the degree of discretion and its consequences for policing communities containing migrants of various motivations, including migrant crooks.

Notes

Include individual human case studies
Portrayal of bigger picture and effects on the economy and social life of London.
Problems of abuse by racketeers exploiting illegal immigrants and those in desperate or tragic circumstances.
Link to smuggling feature.
Maybe a SMUCHII of immigration officers choices—are they multi-choice?
Provide some relics of notorious cases related to immigration.

33　Stop the swindlers

In this feature the visitor should be able to consider and try out police responses to requests for action by the public who have, or think they have, been swindled. This might include complaints of misrepresentation, switching, cut-and-shut, intimidation, embezzlement, fraud, passing off, and so forth. The realities of supporting the victims and the emotional stress these people experience should be included.

Police successes in catching swindlers should also be highlighted.

Educational purpose

To show how swindlers are brought to book, and the police's need for help from the public. Showing the extent to which we are all victims, knowingly or not, of swindlers.

Notes
This is not an amusing subject area, and a dramatically different approach is needed for it to be successful.
Show various ways of approaching the police for help.
SMUCHII opportunities and/or other interactives.
Show past cases with actual objects if available

34.   Disturbance in a pub

Called to a pub disturbance the policeman has to decide what to do and to do it. His actions are guided by his presumptions about what is probably happening. The visitors are seated in the pub (which might sometimes be used for serving private parties). The policeman is prone to misjudgement and prejudice in his actions. Possibly a SMUCHII working by consensus of those in the pub would be amusing.

Educational purpose

To show the difficulties of stopping violence without using violence. To show how easy it is to misunderstand what is happening.
To highlight differences between individual and group views on events.

Notes

Use of concealed speakers to generate noises
Show systems used by pubs to curtail unruly behaviour.

35   Victorian policing

This should use props and a SMUCHII to enable the visitor to experience what it was like to be a Victorian policeman. It is an opportunity for time travel.

A pre-show should tell of Bow Street's police history in the early days of the Met before the present buildings were erected.

The script should draw in some of the key changes in policing over the last 150 years.

Educational purpose

This is a platform for showing the history of the Forces and, more subtly, how policing is in some ways the same and in other ways has changed.

Notes

This should feature some period humour but not in a way that laughs at the Victorians from the present day.
A Victorian shop interior in Bow Street might be replicated as a setting for an incident.
Interesting memorabilia should be available

36 Anti-subversion

This is about how the police find out in advance about the plans of people who are involved in organised subversion of the democratic state or who are prepared to take illegal action for causes such as communism, Ireland, animal rights, suppression of Salman Rushdie's writings, anti Royalty, anti nuclear weapons, road traffic, or their equivalent in earlier times. The people involved are using unacceptable behaviour to achieve political change rather than financial gain. Such people always exist in society and are countered by informers, wire-tapping, bugging, and protection squads. Policing which suppresses them may itself be subversive because it can harm the innocent or lead to a police state if not restrained.

Educational purpose

To show that British policing is not an arm of the state and is guided by the public and controlled to some degree by magistrates. Police do not and cannot always judge correctly the amount of action they need to take. They may be over concerned or under concerned about a particular threat to society.

Notes

This is the kind of subject that would best be tackled in a humorous way.
The actions or alternatives available for the plain-clothes policeman who has infiltrated a cell that is planning violence might be included.
The actions of a police inspector who has to contain a peaceful demonstration that includes activists prepared to take direct action may be an element.
The choice of precautionary arrest?
Demo of intelligence collecting methods.
Probably includes a SMUCHII.
Opportunity to try out bugging and wire-tapping.
Probably lots of memorabilia available.

37 Press conference

Within a room or other space where a real police press conference may sometimes be held the feature should provide visitors with the opportunity to take part in a mock conference. Both composing and delivering information to the press and cameramen in an unbiased way, and answering questions will be an interesting challenge.

There is a possibility of using standard situations for this, with some guideline scripting and some mechanical auto-prompting etc. but the feature is going to be based around the visitors themselves more than most.

Educational purpose

To show how the police keep press and public happy or use them to help find suspects.

Notes

It is in a way all interactive
Role-playing scripts may be required.
Records of past press conferences would be useful, particularly those which have been filmed in their entirety.

38 Stolen property

This should be an interactive feature which provides opportunities for visitors to try out ways of proving ownership of property, and of finding stolen (not lost) property and returning it to the owner. The property may be corporate or government owned as well as personal possessions.
A sense of the dangers to thief and victim should be incorporated.
Causes of theft can be a sideshow.

Educational purpose

The importance of preventing stealing by using property protection measures, which means showing what these are. Use memorable drama to teach visitors the importance of holding proof of ownership.

Notes

The implications of stealing a purse with medication in it might be shown.
List commonly stolen goods
No doubt there are many items of stolen property that have never been reclaimed and maybe some could be included.
There is an issue as to how seriously the police should take minor pilferage, and the merits of zero tolerance. Different cultural groups or even age groups may take different attitudes to this.

39 Raid a premises

In Diamond Bill (feature 12) we see the actual police response to a raid planned by crooks. Here we want to show how the police carefully plan and execute raids to find drugs, arms, counterfeit goods (currency, passports, art, licenses), abused children, and a dangerous murder suspect.
The visitor can be portrayed as one of the team doing the planning and simulating the action, or a more senior policeman reviewing the plans and the subsequent action.

Educational purpose

To reduce the glamour attached to police raids, and show their risks and their impact on the people involved.

Notes

Laughable mistakes, unexpected discoveries and other humorous incidents may be copied from real life.

A many-player SMUCHII is a possible approach. We do not yet know how these things are planned. How many people do the planning and how many purely execute instructions? How many instructions are misunderstood with damaging results and what are the repercussions of this? How does the briefing work? How is leakage of the plan to the criminal community avoided? How is damage minimised?

There will be objects in police possession that were recovered during police raids some may be original or they may need to be replicated.

The equipment used in raids can be available for examination.

19
The rest of the content

In addition to the features described in the last chapter we had decided to include the following fifteen items.

Welcome

The design requirement is to create a very attractive entrance experience that is not institutional in atmosphere. This should start with displays visible from the street, and extend as far as the first part of the exhibition. It should use minimal text and should encompass attraction ticketing and greeting arrangements, live camera coverage of what is happening inside the exhibition, characters, images, lights and sounds to stimulate curiosity and a sense security.

The schools welcome, using a separate entrance and making children feel comfortable and secure, also requires design. There has to be special provision for pre-visits by school teachers.

The use of the exhibition for corporate entertainment for people who may or may not have police connections or interests introduces additional requirements. Again, pre-visits by organisers need special provision.

Personalisation

The purpose of personalisation is to allow visitors to choose, if they so wish, the features which they wish to visit and to direct them to these features in an appropriate sequence which takes account of the need to maximise customer satisfaction and minimise congestion and waiting periods. It is proposed to do this by enabling each visitor to choose a card before or at the entrance which can be bar-coded to provide interactive control information, rapid access to virtual museum material, records of activities which are retrievable on leaving, a souvenir, and possibly an ordering system for the purchase of goods. These cards may be sponsored.

Education Service

A room has to be provided for school parties of all ages, usable for other purposes in the afternoon or evening. This needs to be fitted out with seven adjustable height tables, chairs/stools of suitable sizes for six-year olds upwards, TV monitor, Video/CDRom player, lecture stand, uniform and hat collection for younger children, disguise demonstration equipment, board and computer games, movable bookcases and drawing implement receptacles, white board and movable display boards, lunch box racks and storage for all of these.

No-brainer education packs have to be prepared for children of each age group showing relationship to the national curriculum, the facilities available, suggested visitor programmes, pre-visit teaching material, booking arrangements etc. Also browsing book lists.

Requirements for day to day management and marketing of these facilities, including materials supply to be agreed with Heritage Projects.

Note: It is intended to invite a caterer to provide lunch boxes for children so that they do not need to bring their own food. The supply contract for these including content and price has to be decided prior to inviting tenders

Medals and badges

This is a display task intended to provide those interested with sight of medals and badges used by the Police services at different times. A clear distinction must be made between the six different Police Services.

Briefing room

The room has to be fitted out as for a cinema, with room for personal presentation as well, capacity at least 40. It will normally show short films but may be used for other purposes.

Whose manor?

This feature will show the boundaries of the two police services and their divisions. It will show the policing functions which are the responsibility of these services and of other services such as British Transport Police, Royal Parks Constabulary, Port of Tilbury Police, Ministry of Defence Police, traffic wardens, customs and excise, trading standards and immigration services. Historical changes in these boundaries and services should be included.

In order that this information is noticed by visitors it is necessary to enliven its presentation. The relevance to the citizen of knowing about these matters should be explained. Similarly for the individual police officer.

This exhibit is an opportunity to explain that not all of policing work is the responsibility of the police services and that in some countries the work is divided up in different ways, e.g. traffic police services.

A police box

This requires the procurement and fitting out of a "tardis" type police box for inspection by visitors. There is also a police radio box on offer which might be exhibited.

Humorous touches

These may be of any kind and be placed anywhere. Their design and procurement is required.

Chat with a police officer

Volunteers who may be ex-police officers will be available to give information and advice to visitors. The seating arrangements for this have to be created.

Access to history

A desk where visitors can make historical enquiries, which would be manned by volunteers is required. This would be located within the shop area.

Screens for previewing the virtual museum

These screens and associated seating facilities are to enable visitors to choose and run electronic content which is on sale in the shop but may be wanted for information during visits.

Retailing system

The shop layout needs to provide for the display of gifts and souvenirs (including those bought by children), books, CD-ROMs and Videos, and higher priced goods - some of which will have to be under lock and key. Some, but not all of the goods will be of a specialist nature which cannot be bought in other shops. The proportions of different types of goods may be modified in the light of experience. Their positioning should take account of normal retail experience.

In addition to the usual shop sales there will be an e-retail system, and arrangements within the museum for electronic or physical display and pre-ordering of goods which are then picked up at the exit.

Characters

The characters are intended to be electronic "spokespersons" for THE BEAT who can communicate across all levels free of race, gender or creed stereotyping. They should inform, entertain and amuse. They can be used to handle sensitive issues. They can diffuse the inherent tensions between police and public in a charming way. A single character could become too dominant, and could not cover the whole spectrum. A team of five characters could be used together or separately in many different ways.

These characters would appear on screens in the exhibition, video clips, the Internet, advertisements, and merchandise. Models of the characters at any scale can be displayed and sold.

The characters would speak to visitors and on the digital media, and use body language and props to convey messages. Subject to technical limitations they should answer questions from the public. Multi-lingual capability would be an advantage.

Their educational purpose would be to attract interest in the subject matter, especially among children. To provide a vehicle for learning through dialogue and interactivity, and to circumvent learning blockage arising from formality without dumbing down.

Photo booths and vending machines

Booths sufficient to meet demand for souvenir pictures, with or without items of uniform, background scenes etc., and arrangements for retrieval of pictures are to be provided. The practical requirements and the potential profitability of vending food and drinks need to be explored.

Sketch of the museum shop by Jestico and Whiles

20

The Virtual Museum

When we started the project I was uncertain about the amount of space that would be occupied by old uniforms, badges, equipment and other conventional museum objects. But we knew that there was not going to be enough space for many of these so we started to think about the effectiveness of normal museum displays as a means of communicating information and ideas to visitors..

Our early thoughts were that most of the objects in museums are displayed in glass cases where one cannot touch them, smell them or hear any sound they make, and where the amount of information about them which can be made available to visitors is extremely limited by space constraints. Normally only one side of the object is in view and it is not possible to obtain a very close-up look. In central London the cost of space to display a small object to the public is likely to approach £170 per year in energy, rent and business rates.

In contrast, a digitised image of an object can be viewed from every side, as close up as you like. Its sound can be heard. It takes no space and can be dispatched to any part of the world where there is someone wanting to see it. All available information on the object and linkages to other related objects stored in the same museum or elsewhere can be attached so that they are immediately available. Following this reasoning, we started work on the museum our simple notion when was that it was better to show objects in digitised form than in glass cases and to use the space at Bow Street for visitor experiences related to policing.

This reasoning disregarded the initial costs of digitisation which later we found to work out at several hundred pounds for each object. Moreover, I was unaware of how much it matters to some people to feel the presence of an important historic object close by. It seems that the "I've seen it for myself " excitement is a powerful motivation for visits to leading museums. The museum managements are proud of what they have and want to show off, sometimes without much regard for the cost.

Following this reasoning, our simple notion when we started work on the museum was that it was better to show objects in digitised form than in glass cases and to use the space at Bow Street for visitor experiences related to policing.

Observation within museums soon shows that fewer than 15% read the information provided so carefully for their enlightenment. The words displayed, or the voice-over, are more likely to turn people away than to encourage them to pause and look at the objects on view. The desire to know all about things is not very widespread beyond the world of collectors and curators.. Our subject matter made it very necessary for visitors to take in the story of the objects in view.

The virtual museum we were proposing would be "an electronic storage system dedicated to the records of past events, objects of historic interest, and the pursuit of learning or the arts". It would be started with the electronic store of information required by visitors to The Beat, and would provide the means for easy access thereto whilst they were in the building. Later this would be available at home or school if they bought the CD-Rom or Internet download. The contents would be customised to suit specific target markets such as individual English citizens, tourist visitors to Britain, schools, colleges, writers, police officers, and American and Commonwealth citizens of British extraction. Translation into several languages would be available. Learning would also be possible at several different levels of understanding so that it is neither too easy nor too difficult to stimulate the customers.

The unlimited low cost 'space' in the virtual museum would contain a treasure house of narratives about people or past events, images of buildings and objects, and informed explanations of policing practices. It would show how policing adapts to changes in cultural, economic, social and technical conditions. Altogether this was becoming quite an ambitious project.

It may sound obvious, but could not be taken for granted, that all of the content of the Virtual Museum must be truthful, reliable and acceptable to London Police Education Ltd. Inevitably, the material will cast a light upon the Metropolitan Police and City of London Police. This needs to be a favourable light. This is not a forum for presenting contentious matters unless two or more views can be handled in a balanced and dispassionate way. To avoid offence, the presentation of the content would also need to be discussed with minority cultures before it is finalised.

Feeling that we had a proposal that was both necessary and sensible as a complement to The Beat we began to explore the practicalities. Advice was obtained from Thomas Lisle, Nick Ferenczy, Alastair Dryburgh and David Spaidal The latter is an American specialist in the CD-Rom publication business. Will Baker carried out a substantial market research study and John Stevenson produced a draft business plan for the virtual museum as we thought that it had to be a self-supporting venture and should not draw off funds intended for The Beat.

A promotional CD-Rom

The work proceeded in two directions. The first of these was the production of a CD-Rom for promotional purposes. The idea was to sell it as a taster during the year before The Beat opened, and thereafter to sell it as a souvenir and source of further information to our visitors. Thomas Lisle started work on a demo CD-Rom to be used for raising at least £100,000 to finance this CD-Rom.

Nick Ferenczy pointed out that we had a problem with this idea. If the CD-Rom was to be saleable it would need to include games. These could not be of the "cops and robbers" type, nor a computer board game of the Cluedo type, as either would give the wrong image for The Beat.

It might be a game which was a sampler of what a visitor might find in The Beat, such as a SMUCHII. But this would be difficult because one could not so easily engineer the element of surprise, there would be less impact from the small screen, no 3D props, no big sounds and no audience. Altogether it would be a rather different experience. The only alternative seemed to be to concentrate upon criminal investigation, and accept that it was not typical of The Beat.

Then we met a practical problem. The prototype demo CD-Rom which Thomas sent me did not work on my computer, although other members of the team had no problem. Thomas produced an excellent technical explanation for this problem, but the incident left me uneasy. What would happen if a proportion of the people buying the CD-Rom were unable to run it? Would we face the costs of staffing a permanent support line? Would the purchasers conclude that The Beat might not work either? We could not use for promotion a disc which would not run perfectly in any computer which could play music from a CD-Rom.

The team remained very enthusiastic about a promotional CD-Rom but I became doubtful of its efficacy even if the problems were solved. I felt that we were dipping a toe in the virtual museum water, as others have done, but not doing it properly.

A twin business

More and more we were looking at the Virtual Museum as a twin business, which I called "aboutpolicing.com" and registered as a website. (It was the height of the dot.com boom). I assembled a list of CD-Rom subject matters we might cover. Alan Moss gave us constructive comments before taking the list to London Police Education for general approval. The subjects chosen and the way they would be treated are a little different from the Features in The Beat which are set out in Chapter 16 but not so different as to warrant listing in this book.

I assumed without any apprehension that at the appropriate time we would strike a deal with the Police, through London Police Education, to secure the information and advice that we would need to produce the series. I also assumed that sale of this material would be helpful in attracting visitors to The Beat, and the shop in Bow Street would sell many CD-Roms to visitors.

At first sight this looked like a conventional publishing business using new media in place of print. However, books, films and music all present their material sequentially. The strength of the CD-Rom or website is that information can be handled non-sequentially in a way that is both quick and efficient. One does not have to wait to get to the right place to find out what you want to know. It is not even necessary to confine oneself to a small number of choices as proposed for the SMUCHII. A very large number of choices can be offered, limited only by the imagination of the composer and the diversity of the material available.

This is appropriate for information on policing. Much police activity involves assembling non-sequential information – making links to work out what happened or will happen. One can realistically simulate this process with digitised material, much more easily than in (say) a novel. Will Baker visited stores and websites to see what they were offering in the same market place, and at what price with what margins for the retailer. He found a false market with many producers paying retailers to sell their discs, or at least supplying them at below cost, in order to secure other objectives such as the sale of hardware for games. By far the majority of CD-Roms on sale were either games or formal educational instruction. Our proposal did not fit into either of these groups.

Before making any decision on the way forward I consulted David Spaidal. He was keen on our product for the American market. His views were interesting and useful, but I became more and more certain that the future distribution system for digitised material was going to be the Internet not CD-Rom sales in high streets. The subsequent roll-out of Broadband and Wi-fi has made downloading and live interactivity practical and affordable, and now we are seeing the large internet companies offering internet publishing. It is as well that we hesitated.

It would have been possible for us to switch our creative work from an actual museum requiring a property to a virtual museum based on broadband internet services. The latter could have included our SMUCHII concept which we think might be adapted for home use. It is digitally controlled and run anyway.

Such a museum might include digitised versions of the many police stories and maybe the more interesting objects. There is enormous potential for education. All of this would be backed up with a travelling exhibition, perhaps in a large lorry, that toured the London schools and the tourist spots during holidays.

Policemen's leisure activities at Bow Street.

This photo must have been taken before 1906 as the cellblock behind the men had not had its extra storey added.

21

Adapting the premises

When Alan Moss first showed me the former Police Station in May 1998 I was struck by the contrasts between the fine front elevation, the very dull rear walls and the utilitarian interior. These presented a major problem for its owner. It was not as fine a building as it looked and a great deal would have to be spent before it could have a new use. The police had decided that it was obsolete several years earlier and moved their operations to a new building not far away. For any other use it was just as obsolete. Whilst it was structurally sound, it had to be upgraded or replaced to meet current user needs. In view of its significant history and fine frontage to Bow Street it had very properly been listed Grade 2, and therefore upgrading was more appropriate than replacement. In any case this would be demanded by the planning authority.

The Police could not sell the building because that would have compromised the security of the adjoining Magistrates Court. They had no money to do it up. All they could do was to find someone to take the lease and ensure that the actual user was not likely to be a security risk. For several years they found no-one, and in offering it for the museum they were solving two problems at once.

By lifting this problem off the Police we were doing them a good turn. Our team were used to dealing with such problems, but the Police were not. We had an appropriate use for the building which helped to justify the costs of works. No-one else did. I think that the Receiver, who was responsible for the property knew what a good thing it was for the building to be used as we proposed. Westminster City Council planners were very slow to understand this point, as chapter 23 explains.

[Of course all this changed when in 2002 the Magistrates Courts Service decided to close the Courts and move elsewhere. The combined site of the two properties was now available freehold, there were no special security issues, and the Police had an asset rather than a problem on their hands.]

The side wall of the property – a cellblock – with the door we needed to use for the offices entrance.

Facing page – the rear wall of the Police Station and Courts (part)

Repairs

The property comprises four separate buildings. The largest is the former police station standing three and four storeys above street level, with a tall basement below (see page 171). At the rear there are basement store rooms under a service yard used by vehicles. Facing this yard there are two cell blocks rising one and two stories above street level respectively, with utilities at basement level.

By the time I first looked at these buildings in 1998 they had been empty for four years. The outside walls badly needed cleaning, there was minor deterioration of windows, drain pipes, and other parts of the envelop. The inside was damaged and almost all the services needed replacement. Further deterioration occurred as the years rolled by without any decision on its future. We made plans to deal with all of these problems.

ADAPTING THE PREMISES

A new building

Whilst this refurbishment would have made the building useable again it would have been very difficult to provide the lifts and escapes required for public access as a museum or offices. The costs would have been a prohibitive burden on museum finances without a large subsidy from public funds, which was not available. The solution was to demolish the store rooms and one cell block at the rear and erect a new building to almost double the total floor space without damaging the integrity of the old police station and the original cell block. Therefore, my first step after visiting the site was to introduce it to our architect, Tony Ingram of Jestico and Whiles and ask him to work out how to do this.

Because of my personal and professional interest in old buildings I knew that replication of the existing architecture would not be satisfactory and readily agreed with Tony that a steel and glass structure in a different style would be the right solution. As the existing frontage is ornate the new build should be without ornamentation. Eventually, Tony decided the frame would be of steel, and to use glass, and Portland Stone like that on the frontage, for the external cladding of the main new build but.

The height of the new building was an early issue. We decided to keep this below the roof level of the former police station so that the latter would be visually dominant. This accorded with planning policy, although we met a difference of interpretation as to what exactly was meant by 'below roof level'. After all the main building had roofs at two different levels and the cell blocks were lower still.

Often the roof line of modern buildings is disturbed by the top of lift shafts and air-conditioning plant. It is my view that this is aesthetically unacceptable for an addition of this kind where the old building has no protrusions and I asked Tony to avoid them.

As we went on I tended to discuss with Tony only the features of his design which might cause problems with the planners, or for the museum as tenants. Salmon Harvester and their surveyors discussed the requirements of the kind of office tenants they expected to bring in. Otherwise architectural decisions were left to Tony.

English Heritage officials did not like the earlier proposal by the Police's consultants to extend the building, but thought that a new building in the rear yard was sensible if the integrity of the existing building was maintained, including the whole of the original range of cells on the south side of the yard, and of course the Courts on the north side. The architects responded to this by leaving a gap between old and new

ADAPTING THE PREMISES 163

buildings of two or three metres, and roofing this over in glass. Emergency stairways and exit doors were placed in this space as were the two wall-crawler glass lifts which served the upper floors. For safety reasons there was a light weight bridge between the old and new buildings at each floor level.

Before we presented our plans to London Police Education prior to selection, the architects came up with a sketch design for a new building block which had the block running parallel to Crown Court, the pedestrian street at the back of he property. It was angled to the existing main block, and was lower than the eves. A model showing this were part of our presentation to the selection committee. (See Chapter 4, page 29)

This first idea was improved upon as the work progressed and a much more sophisticated design emerged, as shown on the next three pages.

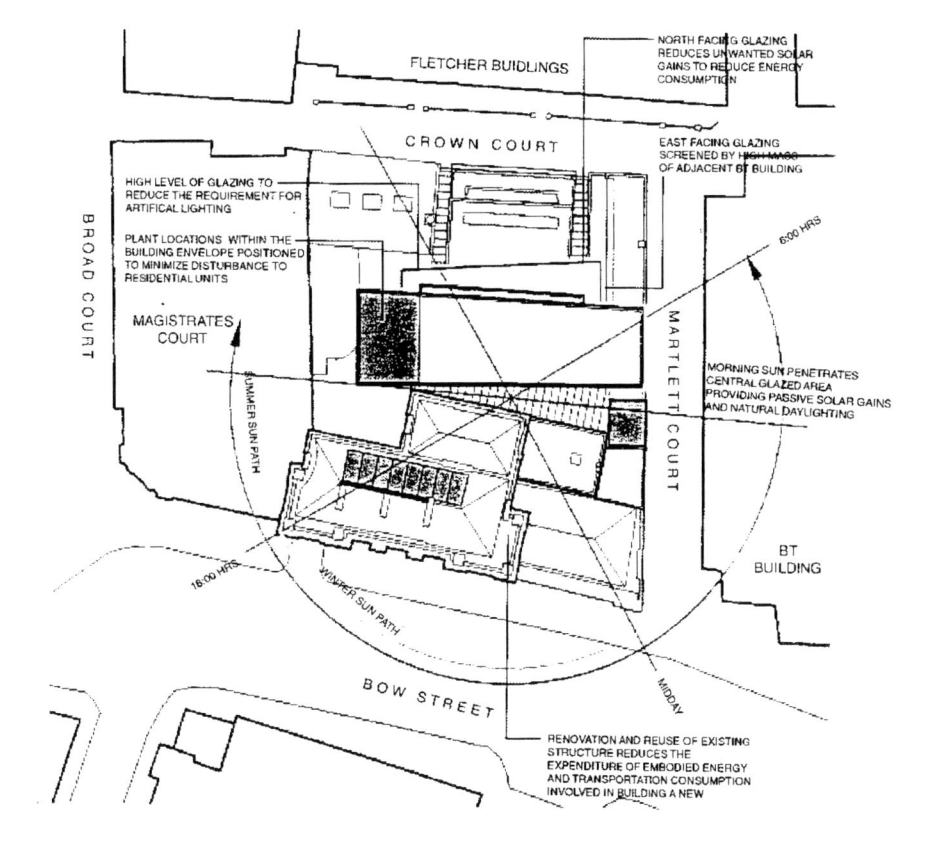

Diagram showing Jestico and Whiles' environmental analysis of the proposal

164 THE MISSING MUSEUM

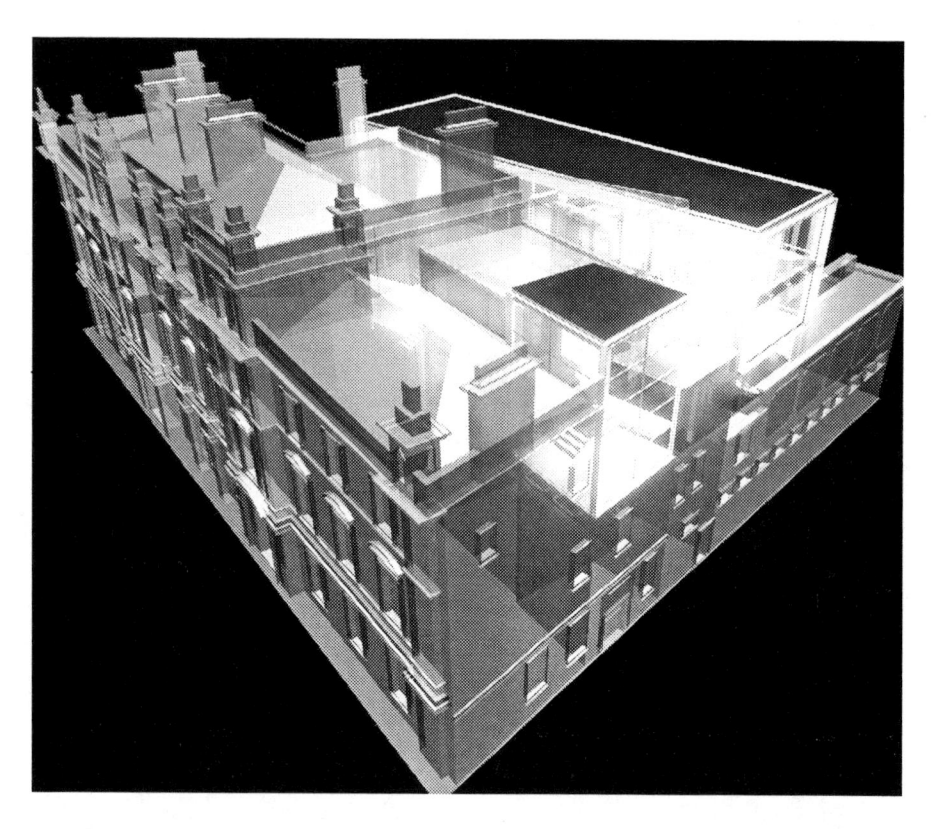

This shows how the main new building sits behind the existing one, and the extension for the stairways fits in at the south end.
Design and image – Jestico and Whiles

It was with great joy that I heard that Jestico and Whiles were pleased with their designs and had submitted them to the selection committee for display at the Royal Academy Summer Exhibition. They had been found distinguished and had been chosen for display. This picture and the two which follow are among those that they showed there.

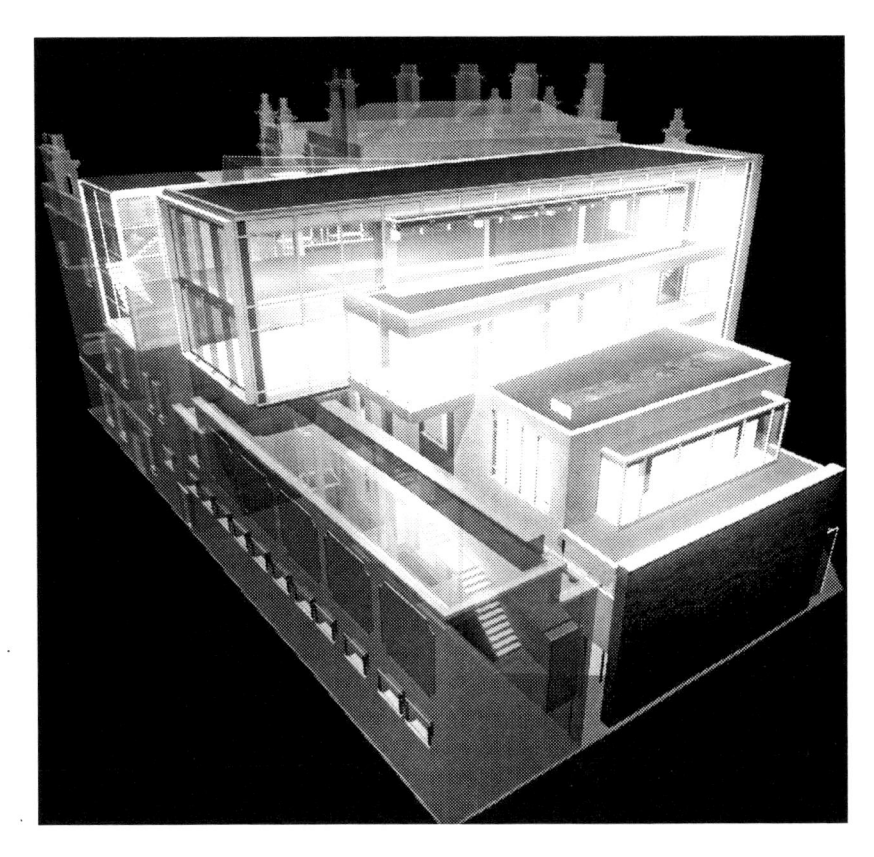

The view from the back, showing the stepping back of
the new building and the way it flies over the cellblock
Design and image – Jestico and Whiles

The final design projected the two uppermost floors of the new building out over the cell block almost to the boundary line of the site. This increased the floor area and in my view it improved the overall appearance by making the building look long rather than tall. It was a feature to which the local planners objected but when we went to appeal the planning inspector found it acceptable.

The view as from the adjoining telephone exchange building .
This show the way in which the new building is connected by bridges
across the gap separating from the old building.
Design and mage - Jestico and Whiles

In order to arrange effective circulation within the offices the architects added a small extension at the upper level of the south wall where in one place the old building did not come out to the site boundary. This extension could be briefly glimpsed from Bow Street and the planners took some persuading that it was acceptable.

In reality, a building in the rear yard is not very noticeable because of the high walls around. The only people it affects are the occupants of the fifty adjoining one bedroom flats, and possibly people sitting by the window in the office block above the adjacent telephone exchange. Our consultant Catherine Morris visited all of the flats and asked the occupants for their views. The result was quite encouraging. These people had been very disturbed by dogs and banging cell doors when the police were using the building. They looked forward to a quiet use of the premises. Loss of light was not a big issue because the daylight was already restricted by residents' deck access ways and flats used electric lights most of the time.

We asked the specialist surveyors, Schatunowski and Brooks to advise on daylight and sunlight consequences for the flats – using the government standards for these. As a consequence of their advice we needed to step back the higher levels of the new building, which meant the development lost some much needed interior space. On the other hand this gave an opportunity to make the building more interesting visually.

The archway from Bow Street used by vehicles to reach the service yard belonged to the Police but the Courts' prison vans were a major user. We proposed a turntable just inside the archway so that they did not have to turn in the yard and we did not lose space needed for the new building. The Magistrates then demanded control over the parking space for security reasons. There is more about our negotiations with the Magistrates in the next chapter.

Throughout the design work we all kept in mind that the outcome had to be of a quality appropriate to a trophy building. We were building to last for centuries, not just a single generation. Advice on costings was provided by the Wheeler Group. The Rolton Group were constantly considering structural and service provision matters. Help was obtained from specialists in acoustics, archaeology, geophysical survey, party wall issues, asbestos surveys etc.

The existing building has high ceilings and we worked out that starting from the basement its five floors were equivalent to six floors with ceilings of an acceptable height for offices, even allowing for raised floors and false ceilings. This gave us an extra floor for offices in the new building. So there would be three floors of offices in both the old and new buildings, all fitted out to a high standard with full air conditioning and IT cabling. Those in the front would have a good view of the Royal Opera House directly opposite.

Access

A secure building like a police station has very few street accesses and making new ones would run counter to its preservation. We had to make considerable compromises to overcome the problem. For instance, we needed to get large numbers of museum visitors in and out of the building, perhaps up to thirty a minute each way, and the front door is only five feet wide, which makes passing difficult. The architects looked at old plans which showed that there had once been another door on the front, and we decided to re-open this. The door to the area at basement level, accessed by steps down from the street, was to be used for school parties.

For the offices we needed another door and the only one large enough was in the side passage known as Martlett Court. (See photo on page 160)

After much anguish about using a side door for prestige offices we decided to use this, improving it as much as possible, and to have a lobby inside which led to lifts up to the office floors.

As there were steps at every outer door we still had a problem with disabled access, and planned small lifts at the office door and a small side door as well as a ramp at the re-opened door.

There were no other doors to the property and we still had to provide fire escapes. Separate staircases were needed up from the basement and down from the upper floors. There were new doors in the rear wall which had to be designed so that no-one could loiter there. They were opposite the flats.

Space for "The Beat"

At first we thought that the museum should be located in the upper floors of the old and new building so that we could use the more valuable ground floor and basement for income generating uses such as restaurants, shops and studio offices. When Salmon Harvester came on to the scene this decision was reviewed and we reversed the arrangement so that offices would take the upper floors. Commercial uses other than high quality offices were excluded from the plans as being less profitable. We kept the museum shop as this is an essential part of a visitor attraction. Exhibition space does not need natural lighting and it must have multiple escape doors to the street, so it suited the lower floors now that these were not needed for shops and restaurants.

We were planning to open up and extend the basement to provide about half of the space for The Beat. This would be connected by a broad staircase and large lift to the old ground floor which would be occupied by the shop and the cells. One corner of the ground floor was to be reserved for the entrance to commercial offices in the upper part of the building, reached mainly by lifts. The rest of the museum space bringing the total to about 1,700 sq.m. would be located on the ground and lower first floor of the new building.

Visitors to The Beat would come in to its shop and ticket desk through the main entrance to the Police Station and leave through the re-opened door on the front. Visitors would circulate freely within The Beat as they wished, as in a supermarket.

Corporate functions might occupy the whole exhibition in the evenings with a finger buffet reception, probably with refreshments laid out in the circulation space on the ground floor or basement near the lift/stairs. Or, one or more of the rooms might be used for this either during the day or when the museum is otherwise closed. Storage areas would be needed for this.

All of this space would be air-conditioned and equipped with lighting points so that the features could be moved or replaced easily. Some features would need walls that were sound or light proofed but these would not be permanent or thick.

The interior

The interior of the police station was austere and functional when built with little detail or decoration. Since construction, many of the original features have been removed or concealed. The fireplaces have been removed and in-filled throughout. The original skirting boards are only evident in a small number of rooms. Dados and cornices had little or no decoration, and have suffered extensive damage from demolitions or service penetrations. The installation of suspended ceilings in most rooms has led to the loss of sections of architrave around many windows.

The ceilings in the main building are supported by simple shallow brick arches resting on cast iron I-sections. In the front part of the building these vaults run between chimney breasts, parallel with the facade. There is a central lengthwise spinal wall to the building. This picks up the load from the lateral ceiling vaults crossing the rear rooms and passages. The fabric, features and finishes within the building have all been altered significantly since construction, particularly at the lower levels. Only one room has remained unchanged through the life of the building.

New partitions have been inserted extensively, the brickwork beside the chimney breasts or from the corridor has been cut away to create new doorways. Most of the doors have been altered or replaced. A flat roofed extension has been built on the top floor.

We were happy to keep original features that were worth keeping, but our requirement was for as much clear space as possible inside the building, for both the exhibition areas and the offices. I was rather taken aback when the conservation specialists from the Council and English Heritage were unhappy about clearing away walls and claimed that the building's architectural significance included its cellular nature. What might they mean?

I was told that it meant that the space was divided into rooms. Given that the room sizes had been changed from time to time and they were now nearly all aesthetically unpleasant tall narrow rooms I felt that this was an argument which had no merit. Vast numbers of buildings have similar rooms and are not listed, so we are not short of examples if we want to see how claustrophobic and inhuman our Victorian inheritance is in this respect.

The compromise was to leave nibs of walls to show where the original walls were, to keep the load bearing cross walls within which there were once large fireplaces, and to retain the central staircase. Original doors, architraves and other detailing had to be kept where they were and the main cellblock was not going to be altered.

Sustainability

The architects sought to reduce energy consumption and hence output of greenhouse gases by their approach to lighting. The gap between old and new buildings was treated as an atrium with white walls which would funnel light into the central depth of the building. The windows were also orientated to bring in light but eliminate direct sun light with its heating burden. The latest high efficiency fluorescent lights were specified, with a lighting control system to dim those at the periphery where natural light could take their place.

There was provision for the recovery of heat in the air leaving the building, and an advanced control system for air conditioning was promised to the planners. Personally I would have liked to do without air-conditioning but the London office market will not accept this, even in a massive old building which heats and cools quite slowly. I quietly resolved to install a minimum of air-conditioning for the floors occupied by The Beat which would have a separate system, and see whether visitors could live with this. It would save money and space.

A challenging task

Before we got near to preparing the town planning submission the architects told me that they were working on their nineteenth version of the scheme! Each version had six floor plans, four elevations and two cross-sections, all to be reconciled. That was a great deal of work for project architect James Tatham and his colleagues.

Whilst I thought that they had produced an excellent design, my main concern by then was essentially practical. We had to be sure that the circulation of The Beat would work and that overall costs were manageable. Engineering, noise impact, and archaeological survey costs had come out higher than expected. The air-conditioning and other services were eating in to valuable space. In the old building, ducting under floors and above ceilings was proving difficult to achieve and there were a variety of lesser problems. A small increase in cost of works is escalated by professional fees and finance costs.

Every few months Paul Stoodley showed me a revised update of his development appraisal and these never seemed to get any better, despite the efforts of Salmon's project manager, Steve Kuntze and their quantity surveyors, Wheelers Group. In the end, if the figures didn't work out we would all have been wasting our time. I was glad to have such good professionals working on the scheme.

Because of my responsibilities as planning consultant to the team and future tenant of half of the development I was very deeply involved in the design process for almost four years, and got to know the details very well. I cannot say that I grew to love the building!

The full front façade of the building

Professional Advisors

Architects	Jestico + Whiles.
Structural and Mechanical Engineers	Rolton Group Ltd.
Solicitors	Lawrence Graham
	Wynne Baxter Godfree
Town Planners	Thorburns
Quantity Surveyors	Wheeler Group Consultancy
Building Surveyors	Matrix Surveys Ltd.
Chartered Surveyors	Weatherall Green and Smith
	Farebrother
	NDH Associates
Development Consultants	WillBeCo Ltd.
Geotechnical Engineers	G B Geotechnics Ltd.
Archaeology	AOC Archaeology
Landscape Architects	Land Use Consultants
Daylighting Consultants	Schatunowski Brooks
Modelmakers	Kandor Modelmakers Ltd.
Acoustics	Cole Jarman Associates
Planning Supervisor	PSK Prout Tilbrook
Police Consultants	London Police Education Ltd.
Project Managers	Salmon Developments plc.
Museum Design	Interactive Science
	Hobson Productions
	Ravest Associates
	Interpretations
	Eigg Ltd.
	Transient
	(others to be selected)
Museum Fit Out	Metropolis AV and FX
	Stevenson Associates
	The Foundry
	(others to be appointed)

22

The magistrates next door

Bow Street Magistrates Courts are in a separate building abutting and having the same architectural style as the Police Station. The two buildings were built together. As explained in Chapter 11, the Bow Street Magistrates Court has long been the premier magistrates' court in Britain. Since an 1870 Act, no other magistrates can deal with extradition proceedings.

We welcomed the Courts' presence because it would help us to advertise the museum. If they fell vacant later we would happily add them to our premises. For their part the Magistrates had no objection to the museum but they were not happy about having to move out temporarily whilst works were in progress. They feared that if they could manage elsewhere for a short period it would be concluded that the Courts could be vacated permanently and they would lose their distinguished, distinctive and historic premises. They also had security worries.

The cells

When I first visited Bow Street it was explained to me that the cell block at the rear of the Police premises was used by the Magistrates Courts daily although it was owned by the Police and was included in the property we were going to lease. The Police promised that the cells would be made available to us, and without them it would have been impossible to achieve a satisfactory development. However, in order to obtain possession of this cell block we would have to replace the cells. If we wished we could provide new cells within our development but everyone agreed that the better alternative was to use spare space within the Magistrates Courts ' custody suite building. This would cost us about £200,000 and the Courts would probably have to close whilst the work was taking place.

Knowing that capital expenditure rules would inhibit this if we paid the cost of this work in cash either to the Police or to the Magistrates Courts Service, I proposed that we carry out the work ourselves whilst completing our project.

So that we could control costs we wanted our architect to design this work in accordance with requirements agreed with the Courts Service. This arrangement was agreed, with considerable benefit to the Courts-although they asked for more! Gradually, the details of the alterations were thrashed out and there was a confidential consultation with the Planning Authority which raised no objection.

Disturbance whilst building

The Magistrates wanted to know when, and for how long, our building works would be taking place as they envisaged that the noise might make it impossible to hear people in Court. On our side, Salmon Harvester were worried about this because they knew that the Magistrates had the power to stop work at any time and doing this would wreak havoc with the project's programme and costs. It became inevitable that if we were to continue the Magistrates would have to vacate their building for nine to twelve months. For this reason they became rather hostile to our scheme, holding up our contract negotiations and formally objecting to the planning permission.

The service yard

The Courts use of the service yard was also a problem It was used by prison vehicles and, I believe, for one staff car. The Service had a wayleave to provide their access through the yard to the prisoner door to the Courts but the yard was owned by the Metropolitan Police and we needed to build there as well as on the site of the cell block. We could see that the Planners might object to this if prison vehicles were no longer able to turn in the yard and had to back in and out.

After considering various alternatives we proposed that we build a secure van dock for one prison van and install a turntable so that vehicles could drive in or out without delays or street blockage. Our small needs for service access, including rubbish removal and bringing in museum exhibits, would be met when the Magistrates were not sitting.

When the Police showed our proposals to the Magistrates they raised objections on security grounds. A specialist security consultant who was employed, I believe, by the Home Office was called in and we had to agree to carry out and pay for some special security arrangements. Their measures included blocking out windows overlooking the turntable and very heavy security doors.. These took security to a far higher level than ever before and probably exposed the lack of security elsewhere in the building, which on several occasions I found quite easy to penetrate without any authority.

The Magistrates insisted they needed complete control of the access at all times, which they had never had before, even though this would have been unacceptable to the planning authority and thus prejudiced the whole scheme. When we tried to restrict it to their operational hours we hit a problem concerning the transfer of control to and from them each day.

Delays

The Metropolitan Police wanted to sort all this out with the Magistrates and we made the mistake of agreeing to this instead of handling negotiations directly. We thought that the two organisations would be on good terms with one another, but found that this was not so.

It took about ten frustrating months and firm personal guidance from The Receiver (who was responsible for both properties) before some kind of compromise was reached. Not a satisfactory or friendly one in my view but we would have got by. A side letter to the lease contract which was to contain provisions for access management was argued about endlessly and never completed.

The questionable delay caused by this tension between two bodies serving the public interest added to our costs and frustrations. As explained in Chapter 6, it led to the property contract being signed by the Metropolitan Police Authority and not The Receiver as originally envisaged. This allowed the Authority to declare the contract void at a later date, whereas The Receiver's decision was fully authorised and would not have been invalid.

Whilst we were waiting for planning permission early in 2002 the Courts Service approached Salmon Harvester to ask if they were interested in buying their building if it became vacant. I advised the Company upon the planning situation, which was going to be difficult as old court rooms have to be preserved. Nothing came of this exploration.

In the outcome, the Magistrates did not keep their courts here. The Courts Service was able in 2005 to sell the building for far more money than would otherwise have been possible. The planning permission which we obtained at our own expense helped them to do this. This capital receipt has gone in to improving other Courts.

23

Un-cooperative planners

Bow Street lies within the City of Westminster, the part of London immediately adjoining the much older City of London on its west side, and containing the Houses of Parliament, two Royal Palaces, the principal shopping streets, hotels, theatres and Scotland Yard, the headquarters of the Metropolitan Police. The City Council's first and most important planning decision would be strategic. Did it want the police museum we proposed in its area? This decision had political, social and economic elements and, as I mentioned in my introduction, it affects the whole of London.

In nearly every place in England and the rest of the world the local authority would have jumped at the opportunity to bring in such a development, for the prestige, the opportunity to show off their heritage, the inflow of money to the local economy, the boost to tourism and the conservation benefits. The red carpet would have been rolled out for us. The fact that the proposal was coming from a charity backed by a public authority and was not a private speculation would have helped even more.

So as soon as we were selected as developers for the project I phoned up the Westminster City Council and asked to speak to the Economic Development officer – an official who usually comes under the direct control of either the Chief Executive or the Director of Planning.

I was put through to a planner who told me that in Westminster there was no such official, no committee which looked at economic and social development issues, and no means of determining the Council's overall view of a project. They did not have a red carpet!

The implication was that we would have to deal separately with the planners, highway managers, building controllers, archaeologists, lawyers, and so forth without any of them knowing the strategic context for their work.

Assuming that the Director of Planning was the chief officer most likely to have a pivotal role in such matters I wrote to him to ask for a meeting setting out our aims as follows;-

1. To restore, preserve and use appropriately a redundant building which is architecturally important and gives character to London, and which stands on an historic site.
2. To improve community relations throughout London by promoting a better understanding of policing tasks of all kinds, among all

ethnic groups – basically by encouraging visitors to try out tasks for themselves in an interactive way;
3. To create about a hundred jobs;
4. To present the story of policing from Bow Street preceding the establishment of the Metropolitan Police and the subsequent experiences of policing London, all of which are an important and little known part of our heritage;
5. To create a visitor attraction of such high quality that it measurably improves Westminster's attractions;
6. To provide a showcase and sale point for selling British manufactured products related to security, law and order.

Wrongly assuming that the project would be welcomed in principle by the Director, I asked to discuss the design concept and details of the new building, that being the main town planning issue, and a procedural point, which was the way in which the proposed uses and access arrangements should be handled in the planning application.

It took an age to get any reply. When I managed to obtain a meeting it was with the officer who had been assigned to deal with our specific case and a lconservation officer. They started off by saying that they were currently seeking further advice upon whether the Police Station might still be required for operational purposes. The statement was confirmed by letter in November 1999 – eleven months after my original letter to start planning negotiations.

This point was quite out of order. The museum would not have been proposed by public advert for this site if the building was not operationally redundant and I could imagine the response of the Commissioner if he had been told that Westminster City Council thought that he was wrong about his operational requirements and so we were not going ahead with the museum! Anyway, in Britain the planning authorities do not have powers to decide the particular use or user for a building – only to refuse a new use if it is materially different from the former use and is harmfully in conflict with town planning principles or policies. This was not the case.

The building's only authorised use is for a police station. Had it been adaptable to suit modern police operations it would have been converted, instead of the Divisional operations being moved to a new building a few streets away. The building cannot be used at all until a new use has been found for it. It has to be preserved and that means a new use has to be found which will generate at least enough income for long term maintenance and repairs.

It seemed to us obvious that if one has to find a new use for an historic building a police museum with closely-related commercial activities is a very appropriate successor to a police station and has no downside. It preserves the historical significance and architecture of the property, and enhances the local tourist economy without harm to local residents. There seemed to be no reason to object to this.

At this first meeting the planners pointed to their written policy which said that if ever the Police Station closed, the property had to have some community use. They did not have any specific use in mind. We thought that the museum was a community use – our second aim in my letter quoted above was to help the community.

Trying to move the meeting on from these two non-points I suggested that for a very long time the main building had been used for offices or for the storage of police equipment. Continuation of these uses with the public coming to see the equipment did not change the use greatly or have any harmful effect upon the neighbours. Some of the cells would need to be kept as they were, and used either for storage or for visitors to see. This argument was not accepted.

The planners went on to paraphrase development plan policy which required new offices to be matched by new residential development, but there was provision for this to be replaced by cultural or entertainment uses including a museum. My interpretation of the rather convoluted wording of these policies is that our proposed uses were acceptable in principle and there was no departure from the Development Plan. The officers said that this was a decision for Members of the Council but I saw this as a formality which need not hold up talks about the design of the new building and internal alterations to the old one.

We did consider residential development. The upper floors of the main building would have made fine luxury flats but the size of the building was not suitable for affordable housing, and the erection of a new building in the yard would make the problem worse not better, bearing in mind that, for security reasons, dwellings would need separate access and escape routes from street level upwards . We were not able to solve these problems even when residential development became more profitable than offices.

The planners asked to see the business plan for the museum so that they could take a view on whether it was viable. To this I responded by questioning their technical competence to review the financial figures. I pointed out that I could not have the figures on their files (which can be seen by the public) because that would have compromised our commercial negotiations. I asked them to nominate a competent leisure professional to examine the document in private and advise them.

We later discovered that they thought we might be planning to have the museum fail within a few years, at which time they would be under irresistible pressure to permit a more lucrative and less desirable use.

Eventually, we obtained a letter from The Metropolitan Police Service which said that if our business failed the museum space would revert to them and not become available to the company which held the head lease. That would take the pressure off Bow Street Partners as operators to fail to continue!

The planners' other points at this time concerned the size of the new building and the internal alterations both of which they thought were too great. These were the issues that the architects and I wanted to talk around, as fellow professionals with shared objectives but not as antagonists. We were keen to narrow down the issues and reach a compromise but they refused to do so on the grounds that the Members had to agree the principle first They said that this could not be done until we submitted our planning application.

In January 2001 I wrote a six page letter to the planning officers which made twenty eight points about the proposal and dealt with all the matters which had been raised. I do not know what happened to this letter as the officers stance did not change and they declined to meet me again until the planning application had been submitted – and for many months after that. None of the contents of my letter reached Members as far as I can see.

Both the architect and I had excellent professional reputations in the field of conservation which we would not have risked for any short term benefit and we knew far more about the building than the planners did.

I have spelt out what happened at this first meeting, later confirmed in writing, because it shows the culture of Westminster Council planners with which we had to contend for the next three years. It did not change when the Council Members agreed the principle of the development. The officers continued to recommend refusal of the application, and to fight it through an appeal which they lost. Sadly, the delays they engendered contributed to the loss of the project.

Public consultation

The site is deeply embedded in an existing community. We arranged to display our proposals to the public and to invite discussion at evening meetings. We also produced three newsletters about the project called "The Runner" and circulated them locally and on the Web. The Police were keen on this approach, helped with copy, and came along to the meetings.

180 THE MISSING MUSEUM

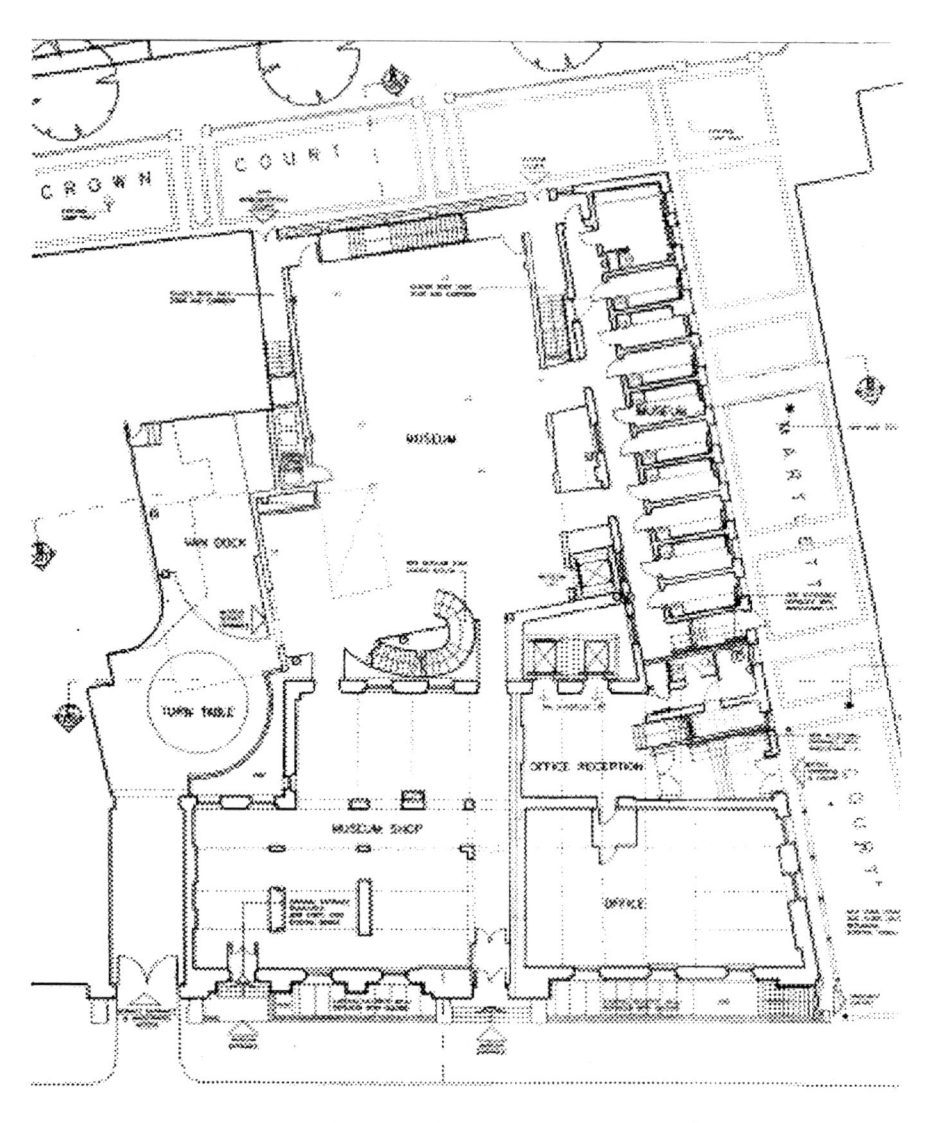

The proposed ground floor layout showing landscaping
in the surrounding foot streets

Martlett Court Residents Association (which represented the adjacent flats) and the Covent Garden Community Association were very helpful in arranging and attending these meetings. I had been a supporter of the latter in its early years, thirty years ago, and I felt our proposal would accord with their aims and purposes. Eventually they became supportive.

Most visitor attractions include a restaurant. We wanted one that would be themed on the police and open to the public passing by. Caterers including Whitbread were very interested in taking the lease but the Covent Garden Community Association and the Council did not want another restaurant in Covent Garden. Local residents voiced strong objections, thinking that it would increase late night drinking in the area. There is no doubt that the restaurant proposal might have become a reason for refusing the application, and we dropped it.

It was obvious that the planning authority would try and extract some public benefit in addition to the museum, either in cash or in kind. Local people said that what they most wanted was the repaving with improved lighting of the pedestrian streets called 'courts' which run around the property. The landscape architects Land Use Consultants were retained to prepare a scheme for this, which would have cost about £150,000 to implement. It is sad that there excellent scheme will not now bring benefits to the local people. (See opposite page)

Listed building consent

The whole project depended upon our obtaining permission to make alterations to the interior of the empty listed building and to clear enough of the lesser buildings to have space to erect an annex to the rear. A main listed building issue turned out to be the preservation of what the experts call the cellular structure and the detailed architectural features within the building.

In Chapter 21 I set out a realistic description of the interior as observed by the architects. There had been so many alterations that preservation was less appropriate than replication of the elements that are appropriate to a high quality building. Yet the conservation team serving the Council seemed, urged on by an officer of English Heritage, to want to prevent the whole scheme going ahead in order to keep something not worth saving. Significantly, a representative of the Victorian Society inspected the building and agreed with us.

New building

For our team the most important challenge was to get right the size and shape of the new building so that it enhanced and did not harm the listed building or the Conservation Area around the site. Without a new building the former Police Station was simply too small for both a viable museum and the commercial development which would pay for it. English Heritage had indicated that they would accept new build in the service yard provided that the integrity of the existing buildings was not compromised. I explained how this was to be done in Chapter 21.

Later on the planners responded by developing an argument that the character of the service yard was being destroyed and the new building should be much smaller, with large spaces on each side. At present the service yard is a miserable space and suggestions that it was a significant courtyard which was once integral to the layout of the whole site was an invention of no merit. A space overshadowed by the walls shown on page 161 is unlikely to be of special merit!

The decision process

The Council was relatively lethargic when we put in our three complementary applications, taking several weeks to carry out routine registration and then doing nothing at all for more than four months except write to statutory consultees. When I could not get a meeting to discuss the revision of listed build details and other issues I wrote to the Director of Planning to complain about the delay, received an appropriate response, and soon afterwards things began to move towards a Council Committee considering the scheme in principle before the details were negotiated.

We had spent some time and effort seeking public support for the planning application, which was forthcoming in a very large number of supportive letters from influential people or organisations. The officers took no notice of this weight of opinion and continued to oppose permission. When we saw their report to Committee in December 2001 I immediately wrote a letter challenging some of the assertions therein, point by point. Alan Moss also wrote on behalf of London Police Education. I expected these letters to lead to some rethinking of the officers advice but that did not happen.

At the Committee the Councillors decided to have a site meeting and that negotiations on our application should continue. So after nine months we were able to discuss details with officers for the first time. When we met them we were disappointed to find that the details of our proposals and letters had not even been digested. The papers we had put in with the application were numerous and complicated in order that we could put over our full case properly. I was not happy about a view being taken based upon peremptory investigation of these. I was expecting to be told precisely what they wanted changed.

Shortly afterwards there was a meeting on site at which Councillors clearly sided with us against their conservation officer – who argued his views fiercely within earshot of one of our team. We agreed to make some detailed amendments to the plans and the amended application then went before a further committee meeting, held almost twelve months after the application was submitted. Three or four months should have been sufficient for handling a case of this kind.

Officers continued to recommend refusal. As the further Committee meeting was about to start I was taken aside by Godfrey Woods, the Area Planning Officer, who told me that there had been last minute lobbying against the scheme and despite new support from such eminent people as Ken Livingstone, the Mayor of London, the applications would be refused but they would invite us to submit a new application with a smaller new building.

Politics

I believe that the Chairman of the Committee had failed to get the application past the controlling Conservative group, whose members included an opponent of the scheme. Whilst Members in favour were the majority of the committee this included Labour Party Members and the Conservatives did not wish to see the proposal go through only with such help. Of course, the secrecy of party politics prevents my ever knowing for sure whether that interpretation is true. It is just what my experience of local government led me to read between the lines. It was perfectly normal party tactics, but it harmed us.

After this it took two months for the Council to issue its decision and we then started to draw up a new set of plans and seek the formal approval of London Police Education, which accepted them, and the Metropolitan Police Authority which never replied. Revised plans were never submitted because we were prohibited by contract from doing so.

The successful appeal

Without new plans to submit, the only possible way of getting permission was for us to appeal to the Secretary of State. On the last day of the six month period allowed for this, which happened to be Christmas Eve, I sent to the Planning Inspectorate comprehensive appeal papers. The appeal process was played out over the ensuing eight months and at the public hearing into the case there were only three points unresolved.

The proposed treatment of the gap between old and new buildings which the planners thought should be wider but the Planning Inspector accepted.

None of the numerous other objections by the Planning Authority had stood up to the close examination which is part of the appeal process. The key issue remaining was whether the new building should be reduced in size in order to preserve the "memory" of the service yard. Given that this would affect the viability of the whole scheme the Inspector thought not.

In September 2003 the Planning Inspector, Ken Barton, granted approval to our plans – as modified internally following original submission so just as I had always envisaged. Godfrey Woods told Tony Ingram that he was gob-smacked. Unfortunately the approval came two years after we should have got it if the Council had acted as other Councils do. It came too late.

24

Abandonment

For the first three months of the year which followed the refusal of our planning and listed building applications we were drawing up new plans and trying to obtain guidance from the planning officers, who said that they still intended to recommend refusal of our new application. They were unwilling or unable to give us much of an indication as to what their Members would be likely to accept. We decided to set back the new build at first floor level and remove the part of the building which extended over the cell block. The museum would lose its upper floor to offset the loss of office space. With reluctance this was agreed by London Police Education as the best available option.

Before we could submit a new planning application we had to obtain the consent of the Metropolitan Police Authority as landlord and our contract required this to be given quickly. Given the response from London Police Education which was supposed to be representing the Metropolitan Police interest, we thought that this would be a formality, as it had been on two previous occasions. The changes had negligible effect upon property values or the interests of the adjoining Magistrates Courts. In July 2002 Salmon Harvester sent the plans to the Authority and asked for approval.

As it was the holiday season and the Property Director had just been replaced by a new man we allowed a little more time than normal before pressing for a reply to our request. We repeatedly requested this during the next six months to no avail. He said that he had not been asked for this although Paul Stoodley, Alan Moss and I were all working from a letter which did just this. No reply was ever received so we could not submit a revised application to the Planning Authority.

This lack of response was a serious breach of contract which was later used by Salmon Harvester as the basis for rescinding the Agreement for Lease.

In my role as town planner I advised that the chances of obtaining approval for a revised planning application would diminish after the local elections the following May and for this reason we needed to put in the revised application before Christmas. As Christmas approached without our being able to do this, I discussed with Paul Stoodley the case for an Appeal and he asked me to put one in so that the project could be recorded in their Company accounts as on-going, and possibly to prevent the contract running out of time. (Its wording was not very precise on this.) We still expected that a new application would overtake the Appeal.

Financial issues

During the summer, Paul Stoodley had become increasingly concerned about the drop in rental values and rise in costs that was going on in Central London. He came up with the idea of delaying the implementation of the scheme until rents had begun to rise again. This would require a change to the Agreement for Lease to allow some discretion as to when works would begin. The existing Agreement required work to start as soon as the lease acquisition was completed. Not knowing of any problems, Paul asked to see the new Property Director, Alan Croney, to discuss this.

After this meeting, which was in September, he reported back to me that he had been questioned about the supposedly low price his firm was going to pay for the head lease and had replied that the amount was influenced by the £3M which was going in to fitting out the museum. Alan Croney said that he did not know about this payment and asked for details. I was surprised at this as it was no secret between myself and London Police Education. As a Director, The Receiver knew all about it and I believed that the information had been passed on to the official handling the property deal.

When I heard of this conversation I realised that Paul's response might have been taken to imply that the museum was being funded indirectly by the Police, which was wrong because we had agreed that we would pay the market price for the property. Paul was not a party to the negotiations which fixed the premium and did not know this. I wrote to Alan Croney to put the record straight.

We had heard by then that the Metropolitan Police Service official who had handled our negotiations in 1999-2000 had been responsible for negotiating another contract where the Authority had sold a property only to see it sold on shortly afterwards at a large profit. (The London property gossips told us which property this was!) Not surprisingly, the Authority's internal auditors had been asked to look at other contracts handled by this official.

I have not been told or allowed to read the result of this internal auditors investigation but deduced from remarks made to me that it had brought to light two financial concerns. The first was that Salmon Harvester might not after all be about to pay a sum which the Authority could sign off as 'best value' on the date the contract was signed. As we thought the contract was legally binding we did not see this as being a problem for us, or being re-negotiable unless a change in other terms of the contract became necessary. Alan Croney thought that re-negotiation was necessary if we proceeded with the revised planning application but our lawyers did not.

The second concern was that under Local Government financial regulations the rent for the museum payable to Salmon Harvester (backed by a rent from us) was a liability which had to be grossed up to its capital value and included in the capital expenditure budget of the Authority – reducing the other capital expenditure which it could carry out within its ceiling. I could understand the problem, and thought that we might overcome it by reducing the rent we paid to the Authority and the identical rent payment by the Authority to Salmon Harvester, and thus lessening the exposure of the Authority. We would pay Salmon Harvester the difference in another way. This idea was agreed with Paul Stoodley and Alan Moss but dismissed by Alan Croney without discussion or explanation.

Due process

When I first met Alan Croney to talk about the situation he emphasised the need to follow due process in sorting things out. As I have never done other than follow due process and believe it is essential in local government I nodded approval.

Where we parted company was over his insistence that he was only concerned with the property contract between the Authority and Salmon Harvester and there was no connection between this and any other contracts or arrangements we might have. I disagreed. Salmon Harvester was not the firm that had agreed to design, finance and operate the museum wanted by the Metropolitan Police and City of London Police. Bow Street Partners Ltd had done that and Salmon Harvester had little or no interest in the museum proposal. The only purpose of the property contract was to facilitate our work so it was ancillary to this.

The law of property might point this way but his view seemed to me to be in conflict with the facts because there was an implicit linkage between the Agreement for Lease and the Endorsement Agreement that was signed earlier with London Police Education acting on behalf of the Metropolitan Police Service. I could make little progress with him and supposed that he had not been fully briefed on the whole project, and how it came about. He insisted that Bow Street Partners had just a down stream interest as tenant. I think he had reversed our roles. This was not how we saw either the contract or the actual situation.

His Department's exposure on the matter of a low lease premium was a problem if he did not act very carefully. Possibly the best thing that could happen as far a he was concerned was for the contract to run out of time, or Salmon Harvester to pull out. But the effect of his actions was to remove from me the key role I had had throughout the project in sorting out difficulties informally and quite openly, without which we would not have been there at all. Alan Moss could see that I should go on with my role and was himself feeling excluded although he had been appointed as co-ordinator of police interests in all matters except the detail of property negotiations. He and I were both very concerned by now.

No information

It seemed to me that the Police interest was now represented by two voices, with different and conflicting agendas. As I had only agreed to take on the project if this did not happen I sought a meeting with the Assistant Commissioner of the Metropolitan Police who had just taken over as chairman of London Police Education. This was arranged and then cancelled by him and I never did get to meet him. Alan Moss told me that he too was not quite sure what was going on.

As the Autumn wore on with no progress I was receiving an increasing number of phone calls from members of our team asking what was happening. They needed to plan their work for the next year. I could not tell them very much lest they get the impression that the project was dead – which would have meant that if it went on I would probably have had to assemble a new team. Creative people do not like being mucked about.

On 19th November I received two letters. One was from London Police Education to say that the Board had discussed the situation and were worried about the delay. A Board Member who was a Member of the Metropolitan Police Authority had expressed his strong personal support for the project and indicated that he wanted the matter brought to the Finance Committee of that Authority as soon as possible. He wished to resolve difficulties with the utmost speed. This letter also asked me to update the financial projections for the museum, was generally encouraging, and avoided giving me full details of the discussions at the meeting.

The other letter was from Alan Croney who said that he spoke directly for the Metropolitan Police Authority and thus confirmed that the Police were speaking with two voices. He started by reporting that he had no evidence that the Receiver ever appointed London Police Education to act on his behalf in selecting a preferred developer. My thought was that this was denying us our status and, if he was right in law that this had not happened we had been misled or at least misinformed from the start. As the Receiver was present when we were interviewed and I heard him say that the property would be made available, I was surprised that any doubt about this could exist and supposed that there was no written record available, although later I found out there was.

A further point in the letter was that a question of "*vires*" was being pursued by the Authority – but Alan Croney was prepared to continue discussions in the meantime. (I assumed that he meant discussions on a revised contract.) This was the first time we heard of their being a *vires* issue. A few days later Alan Moss told me that the officers were investigating whether there was specific authority for the Police Authority to promote a public museum.

Alan subsequently obtained some legal advice on this which I have not seen. From minutes I was later sent I gather that it indicated that there was no legal power for the Authority to provide an historic museum but it could educate the public in policing matters – which was the main thrust of our "museum" anyway. This took us back to the legal interpretation of the word "museum" which was discussed in Chapter 13. I could understand that the officers of the Authority, none of whom had been there at the beginning, might not have addressed this point – and so it turned out, for as far as I can discover the barrister they consulted was not briefed to advise on it. By the time that the situation was reported to London Police Education its Directors appointed by the Metropolitan Police Authority had ceased to attend its meetings, or had resigned.

Meanwhile I continued to press for progress until, in February 2003, I received a letter from The Clerk to the Metropolitan Police Authority which said that it was seeking legal advice upon fundamental questions as to whether the Authority has exceeded its powers. We could not deduce from this what the problem was and had to wait two months to find out. No officer would talk with us. We were kept wholly in the dark.

Sensing that there was no future for the project Alan Moss decided in February to resign as Secretary of London Police Education. He told his Board and us that he no longer had the contacts within the organisation he needed to perform that role.

We heard of another property coming to the market in Central London that might be suitable for the museum and we asked London Police Education if the Endorsement Agreement could be transferred to another site. No reply was received.

In April 2003, Salmon Harvester and Bow Street Partners received letters which said that the Authority did not have the power to enter in to the Agreement for Lease we had all signed in January 2001, and it was therefore void. The project could not continue.

25

Plod's law

After all that we had done for the London Police to take their project forward my colleagues and I were upset by the way in which Paul Stoodley and I were treated during the period of uncertainty which I have described in the last chapter. It was so very different from our earlier encounters with the people who are at the top of this public service. I think it set a poor example to others seeking cooperation between public and private interests. This is of wider importance than our project. We are all human and naturally this treatment made much more difficult for everyone the negotiations that were necessary after the Authority had declared its position.

When we heard that the Authority had decided that it did not have the legal power to set up a museum I thought of all the other Police Forces in Britain who ran such museums and wondered how it could be so. Both Paul Stoodley and I asked for a clarification meeting. These meetings were held separately because our legal positions were different.

Will Baker and I were met by the Clerk and Treasurer of the Authority. We were told that the key issue was that the lease premium to be paid for the property was about £3M short of the market value at the time when the Agreement for Lease was signed and that this meant the Authority was paying a similar sum towards creating the museum, which it did not have the power to do. Had the amount been quite small they would have had the power under a different Act of Parliament.

Our response was that the price had been the market value when the deal was done and we doubted that it had changed as much as alleged between that day and the day of signature. There were plenty of papers on file showing that this had always been the basis upon which the project was going ahead.

We were given copies of a legal Opinion that the Metropolitan Police Authority had obtained from James Goudie QC, and his Brief. In lay language, his principal argument was that the Police Authority had not been given by Parliament the power to spend money on providing a public museum and whilst there was no direct precedent in past cases he produced case law which seemed to him to be relevant. It followed that unless Salmon Harvester was paying open market value for the lease of the property there was a payment for the museum wrapped in to the deal, which made the contract void. There was no way around this if the amount of shortfall below market value was substantial.

We were not ourselves competent to challenge his legal argument but went carefully through the facts that were used in forming the Opinion and found that there were a considerable number of errors. These would not have been Mr Goudie's fault, but that of those who briefed him and I knew that these people had neither been conversant with the details, nor had they consulted upon them with people like Alan Moss and myself who knew them.

The Authority had commissioned a retrospective valuation of the lease interest to find out how large the financial shortfall was and we were given a copy of this too. Paul Stoodley and I went through it carefully and found that the costs of construction work had been considerably underestimated. We had quantity surveyor estimates for that date and the valuers did not ask to see these or carry out their own surveys. The planning assumptions that had been used to decide what planning permission was likely to be forthcoming were wrong. For instance, they assumed that permission would have been given for a restaurant, which was contrary to the planner's advice at the time. They also assumed that the whole building could be used for offices and ignored the community use requirement of the planning authority.

It seemed that the planners' advice which we had copied to London Police Education as we went along had not been found on the files and passed to the valuers. Therefore the Authority had made assumptions based upon the situation eighteen months later by which time the Planning Authority had changed its position substantially. A big overvaluation would have been the result.

There was another point that the Authority had not taken in to account. Property values in London fluctuate and hence a valuation in a particular month may be higher or lower than the medium term trend line. Some discretion in interpreting valuations is needed if one is working on a project with a long lead time. A retrospective spot valuation is only part of the story.

Salmon Harvester pointed out that before the Agreement for Lease was signed their lawyers had asked for and received a specific assurance by the lawyers acting for the Authority that it had the power to complete the contract. In short the company had been misled about this and hence the Authority had been negligent.

Local authorities and void contracts

It was two years later that I found out why the law allowed this voiding of an agreement at all. One would have thought that a contract that had been signed was binding, whether or not the parties had power to enter into it. That is, I am told, the position for contracts between private parties and used to be the position for local authorities until two months before we signed our contract. That the law had been changed by a court case in November 2000 was unknown by most lawyers at that time because details of the change in the law were not published for many months. (The case is called Hackney ex p. Structadene)

The newly interpreted law is that a local authority does not have to proceed with an unlawful contract unless and until the transaction has been completed, which in our case did not happen. The reality now is that the private purchaser who spends money drawing up plans, getting planning permission or for any other purpose is at risk until the land acquisition transaction is completed. This is obviously a disincentive to a public/private partnership where planning permission has to be obtained before completion.

We have not found any similar case to our own. There is no precedent to guide subsequent actions.

Our options

At this point in time, May 2003, Salmon Harvester and Bow Street Partners had four options. We could resignedly walk away and do something else, we could try to get a court to restore the contract, we could try to get compensation despite being told that the Authority had no power to pay any, or we could try to negotiate another contract. The Metropolitan Police Authority said that it was not interested in anything but our walking away quietly, which told us something about its stance.

Bow Street Partners felt that it could not walk away from the project. It had no significant assets and owed a considerable amount of money to consultants who had been willing to work in advance of payment because they trusted both the Police and Bow Street Partners and thought they would do what they said. Will Baker and I felt obliged not to let these people down, regardless of our own feelings. In addition, we had asked Salmon Harvester to help us with the project and felt duty bound to help them.

Salmon Harvester discussed the options with us and took legal advice before deciding to claim against the Authority for negligent misrepresentation based on the assurance it had been given. It sought recovery of all its expenditure on the project but the law precluded its obtaining any compensation for loss of the contract and the opportunity it gave to make money. Bow Street Partners reluctantly accepted Salmon Harvester's decision to rescind the contract (that was said to be void) on the grounds of breach of contract but persuaded it not to confirm that the contract was void, thus allowing us to test that contention in court if we wished.

The Metropolitan Police Authority asked the High Court to strike out Salmon Harvester's action but was unsuccessful and had to pay the Company's costs. During this case Salmon Harvester changed its position and agreed that the contract was void, which was not helpful to Bow Street Partners' position. After this the legal processes slowly continued towards a date for a hearing and I was asked by the Company to help with evidence. In 2005 the Authority agreed an out of court settlement. I do not know any details of this.

Bow Street Partners took legal advice which indicated that we might not be able to pursue the same line of argument but that the Authority would want to settle any liability to us at the same time as it settled with Salmon Harvester. We were advised to "sit on our hands" for a while, whilst the proceedings went forward and no decision was made about initiating court action. However, we were warned that if we started proceedings we would be asked to pay into court a very large sum to cover the costs of the other side if we lost. Losing would cost us about £250,000. In other words we were up against the superior assets of a large public authority without a remedy if they reneged on a contract where the law had not been fully explored.

Seeking a new contract

In September 2003 I came back from holiday to find that we had won the Planning Appeal and now had planning permission. Also, the Government had issued to local authorities a general power to sell properties at up to £2M below market value if there were good economic or social reasons for doing so. Believing that there were such reasons I wrote to ask for a new contract to be explored which would use up-to-date values and correct assumptions. I got a brush-off which suggested to me that the Authority had reasons other than the legal problem for dropping the project.

A further opportunity for the project's revival came a year later when the property was put on the market along with the Magistrates Court. I was approached by two young businessmen who had sold their business and wanted to use the proceeds to create a police "attraction" in Bow Street. At first they knew nothing of our venture. After I helped them with their business planning they raised money to buy the building, put in a reasonable offer, and asked to meet representatives of the Authority. This could, I believe, have been an acceptable way of continuing the project without acting illegally although my role would have changed. They told me that they could not get a meeting.

At any time it would have been possible for the Authority to seek Ministerial approval to sell at less than 'best value' and given the history of the case and the arguments for the museum this might have been forthcoming. The only conclusion I can reach is that regardless of the legal problem over the existing contract the Authority had no interest in continuing with the museum project.

It seemed to me that ithe Authotity was in breach of the partnership agreement we had with London Police Education which had been asked to act on its behalf. Sadly, that charity turned out not to have the position stated in the original advertisement and was unable to take action on the problem despite the high standing of its Board Members.

I had sent the Authority a summary of all that had happened on the project since the beginning, and I now put together a complaint and sent it to the Chairman. I asked for a meeting to discuss the situation and see if there was a way forward. He declined to meet me (possibly upon legal advice) but he indicated in a letter that the Authority would reimburse some of the costs we had incurred. We were asked to provide a schedule of these but when we sent this in we received a stalling reply from solicitors saying that the Authority would do nothing until the Salmon Harvester case was resolved. I do not know why.

There was no compensation available for our five years of effort, or our lost opportunities to make a profit from the project, or the alternative opportunities we had passed up whilst working on the project. No-one suggested that we had done anything wrong – it was simply a raw deal for us which could not have foreseen.

Re-instatement of the Agreement for Lease

We still had the option of trying to reinstate the contract by taking the Metropolitan Police Authority to court to show that it was not *ultra vires*. There was no other way of getting the decision reviewed or changed. This is because of the way local authorities work. Once their barrister had shown that he could develop a case based on precedent which showed that it did not have power to enter in to this contract the Members of the Authority would have been personally at risk of being surcharged had they proceeded with it to completion. They would never take that risk.

I think we can take this point back somewhat further to before the barrister was briefed. Once the officers of the Authority were alerted to this possibility they could not have ignored it. It would have been obvious that if they found a good lawyer who specialises in this area and briefed him about their concerns he might have been equivocal but there was little likelihood of his saying for certain that the contract was legal. So the real point of decision came when the Authority sought a barrister's opinion, not when the Members heard his learned reasoning. I think that had we been told of the doubt at the time and invited to agree the Brief we would have ensured that it was factually correct and saved many months of uncertainty for our team.

Put another way, the Metropolitan Police Authority obtained the opinion of a prominent lawyer on a matter which has never been to court. He identified the arguments which he would have used in court to try to establish that his client did not have the power to proceed with the contract. He was not acting as a judge and his points were never tested. Our counter-arguments were not considered because once he had voiced his opinion there was a doubt. Members and Officers of the Authority would have been personally liable for the misuse of public funds if they had fulfilled their contractual obligations without proper powers. It was too late.

In law, the 'best value' price for a property relates to the date when the contract is signed and not when the deal is agreed. In this case there was a twenty month gap between the two. The lease premium to be paid was agreed in May 1999, at which time it was considered by the Receiver and myself to be market value. The amount was deduced from a previous valuation by Donaldsons and known changes in building costs and rents. The Receiver had also taken advice from valuers and decided that my offer was sufficiently in line with their figures to be an acceptable approximation to market value. I was told, but have no proof, that this was confirmed by the Home Office and the Treasury.

Due to the Magistrates objections and the arrival on the scene of the Metropolitan Police Authority the contract had not been signed until January 2001 by which time the value had, it was now alleged, more than doubled. We subsequently found out that in May 2000 the Receiver had been alert to the possibility that the value might have risen and had minuted that he had advised London Police Education that it was not a problem at that time.

The Metropolitan Police Authority took ownership of the property just two months after this but made no attempt to check the value or to obtain the Minister's consent to lease the property at below best value. Perhaps they were happy that The Receivers view in May 2000 still applied. Perhaps it was an administrative oversight.

The end

In July 2004 the property was put on to the market together with the Magistrates Courts next door even though no settlement had been agreed with Salmon Harvester or Bow Street Partners, both of whom had registered their interest with the Land Registry. I received fierce letters from the Authority's two firms of solicitors which cautioned against holding up the sale, although I do not think we could, or did, do so. I complained to the Clerk and eventually the Authority made Bow Street Partners a payment towards its abortive expenditure, which was passed on to our consultants.

What was there in it for the Authority?

The sale was completed in the summer of 2005. The Financial Times reported the sale price as £10M but the Authority has not confirmed this. Our own calculation led us to believe that this was about the market value in 2005 but only if planning permission is obtained for its conversion to a profitable new use.

If the figure is correct and the Magistrates Courts Service received its share the amount of money received by the Police Authority does not come to very much more than we were going to pay, after legal fees and payments to Salmon Harvester and Bow Street Partners. One might think that this was not enough to justify the abandonment of a useful project, even though it could be more than we would have paid. Maybe they got more, and the F.T. is wrong.

Throughout the two and a half years of strife on the abandonment of the project we did not discover the motives of the Metropolitan Police Authority. Officials had told us that it simply did not have the power to proceed, but we know that this view depends upon a grey area of law, and a valuation and legal Opinion that somehow adopted some questionable facts. We also know that the normal practice of local authorities faced with a void contract is to try to replace it with a good contract of some kind, seeking Ministerial approval of this if necessary.

No move was made by the Authority to discuss the possibility of a new property contract with either London Police Education or our consortium. The four people who had negotiated the original contract were The Receiver who had moved on, an official who no longer worked for the Auhority, Alan Moss and myself. Three of us were not consulted upon what was happening. I have not asked the former Receiver.

This was unusual. Bow Street Partners Ltd. had been chosen through competition to be the preferred private sector partner of the two London police forces acting through London Police Education Ltd., a responsible charity subject to charity laws and procedures. It seemed that one Police Force could set this all aside without even consulting the other Force, or London Police Education, or our consortium.

There are four possible reasons for this behaviour:-
- One or more mistakes had been made, perhaps in 2001 or when the contract was breached, which the Authority wanted to bury.
- The Metropolitan Police no longer wanted the museum. Maybe this was for security reasons following the events of 9/11, or for some other reason we do not know about. Officials assured me that this was not the case, but I did not hear the views of any senior police officer, whereas the Metropolitan Police Commissioner when we started, Lord Condon, was always strongly supportive of the project. It probably wasn't the view of the City of London Police for they behaved like aggrieved bystanders in the dispute.
- The decision by the Magistrates Courts Service to leave and sell its adjoining premises has removed the need for police control over the property, and added to its value. Our planning permission had also enhanced its value. The liability for looking after a listed building for which it was difficult to find an acceptable use could now be off-loaded, whereas it could not in 1997 or 2001. The Authority could rid itself of a problem.
- The Metropolitan Police wanted to sell the property for as much money as possible, and thought it could get more than we were offering. If so, it considered its short term budget more important than its heritage, or the benefits to policing London which would have come from the project.

****

INDEX

A

aboutpolicing.com 158
access 71, 135, 154, 169
accident signs 137
admission charges 22
Advanced Thinking Systems 94, 101
Adventure Projects. 30
advertisement 7
air conditioning 22, 169, 172
aliens 78, 118
Aliens Registration Office 48, 78, 127
American 157, 159
ancestral home 79
animal rights 148
antiquities 82, 83, 111
anti-subversion 148
appeal 185
archaeological survey 25, 172
arrest 102, 106, 114, 123, 148
Aspirations 4, 100, 103, 108
ARPO 59
attractions 17
audio-video 89, 90
auditors 188
authenticity 7, 81, 90
award winning 11, 77
AYH 30

B

basic task 62
battle 78, 120, 139
Belisha beacons 131
benign 60
'best value' 188, 196, 197
Black Christian Civic Forum 5, 51, 56

Black Maria 114
Black Museum 15, 16, 141
Blue Lamps 5, 30, 84
boats 134
Bob Melling 3, 83, 97
Bow Street Magistrates Court 73
Bow Street Police Office 74
Bow Street Runners 7, 73, 74, 116
bravery 139
budget 23, 37, 38, 39, 45, 94, 99, 100, 189, 199
bugging 148
building alteration 25
bullet-proof vest 121
business plan 22-25, 39, 157, 180

C

cameras 69, 131, 134, 143
capital expenditure 44, 175, 189
capital punishment 117
car chase 131
cargoes 134
cartoons 112, 117, 131
Catherine Morris 3, 97, 168
CCTV 89, 103, 143
CD-Rom (s) 92, 154, 157-9
characters 95, 152, 154, 155
Charlies 73
Charlton 10, 15, 111
chase 103, 143
children 18, 22, 53, 54, 55, 56, 59, 82, 86, 87, 92, 119, 131, 151, 152, 153, 154, 155
Choudhury 51
citations 139
clues 102, 122, 123
collection 7, 10, 15, 79, 83, 111, 113, 152
colonies 141
Commissioning 98
Commonwealth 157

Community service order 141
community use 39, 180, 193
compensation 194, 196
constable 69, 106
control room 89, 115, 121, 143
conviction 103, 141
cooling plant 22
corporate entertainment 54, 152
corrupt 73, 74, 138
counterfeit 138, 151
counterfeit 138
court room 120
courtroom 80, 120
Courts Service 42, 161, 175, 177, 198, 199
Covent Garden Community Association 183
crashes 132
cultural communities 127
custody suite 74, 79, 175
customs officer 125

D

David Spaidal 157, 159
Davis Coffer Lyon 25
day patrol 75
daylight 43, 168, 169
decisive moment 123
definition 83
demonstrations 70, 121
design team 7, 35, 56, 59, 95
development appraisal 24
Development Plan 180
diamond 102, 124, 151
digitisation 156
digitised image 156
disabled access 170
disguises 136
disturbance whilst building 176
divers 134
dog's eye view 140

dogs 15, 80, 97, 102, 107, 130, 139, 168
domestic 80, 87, 140
drug 103, 140
due process 189
Duke of Bedford 73, 74, 75

E

education 60, 85, 101, 110, 153, 159
electronic eyeballing 136
emergency calls 142
emotional 60, 80, 88, 90, 109, 127, 137, 141, 145
emotions 60, 61, 80, 99, 109, 119, 120, 126, 133, 140
enactment 120
English Tourism Council 17
enquiry point 119
entrance experience 152
environmental analysis 5, 165
ethnic communities 46
exhibition centre 82
eyewitness 111, 122

F

façade 5, 77, 173
Falana 3, 51
Farebrother 25
features 5, 13, 23, 56, 62, 68, 79, 89, 92, 93, 95, 97, 98, 100, 102, 104, 106, 111- 113, 117, 140, 152, 164, 171, 183
fencing 138
film 12, 20, 21, 38, 124
financial concerns 188
fingerprints 70, 122
flight 90, 128
foot patrol 74
forensic 122, 136, 138
forgers 138

fraud 103
freedom of speech 121
freehold 24, 43, 76, 161
Friends of the Historical
  Museum 59, 79
fugitive 103, 140
functions 13, 21, 45, 54, 69, 81, 153, 171

G

gallantry 139
Galleries of Justice 16
gaolers 141
gas canister 113
George Smith and Co 76
Gordon Riots 74
graphics 93, 95
greeting 152
ground floor 5, 32, 77, 81, 170, 171, 182
gun control 117
guns 16, 133, 139

H

handcuffs 113, 114
helicopter 89, 102, 104, 128
helmet 85, 113
Hendon Police College 15
heritage 107, 108, 111, 118, 178, 179, 199
Heritage Projects 3, 11, 12, 23, 24, 28, 35, 42, 45, 91, 94, 101, 153
heroin addicts 106
high collar 113
historical enquiries 154
historical period 88
history 18, 102, 114, 115, 118, 126
Home Office 39, 75, 176, 197

horse 69, 75, 88, 102, 113, 126, 131
horse patrols 75
humour 112, 134, 137, 139, 141

I

Ian Russell 3, 61, 88, 90, 92, 98
identification 46, 123, 136
Identikit 136
identity 47, 103, 123, 127, 136
illegal immigrants 84, 87, 144
illegal substances 129
imagery 93
immersive experience 57, 90
immigration officer 144
infiltration 124
intelligence led 103
intelligence systems 133
intelligence–led 133
Intelligence-led 133
interactivity 17
interior 5, 9, 25, 26, 31, 77, 78, 79, 106, 112, 118, 128, 132, 147, 161, 169, 171, 183
issues 46, 56, 68, 82, 94, 99, 101, 110, 121, 155, 161, 169, 178, 181, 184, 188

J

J.G.Ballard 98
Jestico and Whiles 2, 3, 11, 31, 155, 164, 165, 166, 167, 168
John Fielding 74, 75
John Stevenson 3, 16, 94, 124, 157
judgements 110
Julian Ravest 3, 83, 91, 92

L

Lance Bohl 3, 93, 98
landscaping 182

languages 52
law and order 18, 108, 119, 127, 179
layout 76
lease acquisition 188
legal Opinion 192, 198
leisure activities 5, 160
linkages 156
London Dungeon 13, 16
London Transport Museum 17, 18, 21
Lundwich 26

M

main entrance 19
Manchester 16
market value 38
marketing plan 101
Martlett Court 77, 78, 170, 183
matrons 77
measuring 129
medals 113, 139, 153
memorabilia 7, 8, 10, 79, 80, 94, 111, 113, 128, 131, 134, 136, 142, 147, 148
merchandising 101
messages 61
Metropolis AV+FX 11, 91
Michael Hobson 3, 88, 92
migrant crooks 144
migrants 127, 144
misrepresentation 145, 194
Mission Statements 67
Monopoly 73
mounted policing 126
Mowlem 3, 11, 25, 27, 35, 37, 40
multi-lingual 92, 115, 117, 127
museum arrangement 81
museum concept 80
museum of incidents' 8
must see 18, 53, 59, 82

N

Neighbourhood Watch 46
new building 27, 30, 43, 79, 81, 97, 161, 164, 165, 166, 167, 168, 169, 170, 179, 180, 181, 183, 184, 185, 186
NFU Mutual 41
Nick Ferenczy 3, 88, 92, 157, 158
Northcroft 11, 25, 27, 41
notebook 122

O

obsolete 161
officer discretion 114, 125
operating costs 8, 12
optimum 112
organic change 112
ornamental character 77
ornamentation 164
overcrowding 55

P

parades 121
personalisation 109, 152
plain-clothes 148
Point Duty 131
police car 132
police cars 131, 132
police complaint 103, 135
police office 118
political change 148
politics 185
posters 113, 125
precedent 192, 194, 196
premium 24, 42, 188, 190, 192, 197
press conference 103, 149
pre-visits 152
prison visitors 141
private sector partner 1, 38, 42, 198

project manager 13, 173
property protection 150
property values 30, 39, 187
pub disturbance 146
public benefit 83, 183
public consultation 181
publishing 159
punishment 16, 69, 71, 116, 141

Q

quality 101, 112
queues 104

R

racism 46, 49
racist 47
racketeers 144
raid 103, 151
railways 84
rapid response 128, 134
rear walls 161
recruitment 53
regimental museum 59
Repairs 162
residential development 30, 180
residents 48, 54, 83, 101, 118, 127, 128, 169, 180, 183
restaurant 12, 25, 39, 183, 193
retailing 55, 101
revised application 187
riding 126
river police 15, 62, 134
road accident 137
robust 23, 94
role-play 120
Rolton 3, 95, 169
rowdy crowd 87
Royal Academy 18, 166
Royal Opera House 7, 9, 73, 74, 169
royalty 22, 59

S

Sam Burford 3, 85, 95
Sampson Wright 74
scenarios 68
school parties 21, 23, 53, 81, 152, 170
schools 10, 53, 57, 59, 61, 88, 92, 110, 152, 157, 160
science centre 60
section house 77, 78, 118
sensitivity tests 22
sentencing 103, 141
Sherlock Holmes 16
shop 5, 17, 23, 45, 56, 57, 81, 101, 104, 106, 147, 154, 155, 159, 170
shoplifter 143
short measure 129
side wall 162
signage 93, 100, 112, 131
Simon Harris 3, 91, 98
Sir Henry Fielding 74
Sir John Taylor 76
Sir Reginald Mayne 116
Sir Robert Peel 75
slow progress 43
smuggling 84, 125, 144
smuggling 125
social development 178
social research 104, 108
souvenir pictures 155
specifications 93, 94
state violence 98
stolen property 103
stone frontage 106
stop-and-search 127
street fight 88
structure 22, 25, 27, 30, 83, 110, 118, 164, 183
subsidy 164
suffragettes 77

sunlight	43, 169		
suppressing dissent	48		
surcharged	196		
suspicious behaviour	46, 47		
sustainability	22		
Sustainability	172		
swindlers	145		
sword	113		

T

talking head	114, 115
tardis	154
target markets	108, 157
targets	51, 53, 55, 143
tear gas	88
terrorists	103, 117
The Police Gazette	75
The Runner	79, 93, 181
Theatre Museum	17, 18
theft	133, 150
Thomas de Veil	48, 71, 73, 74
Thomas Lisle	3, 92, 157, 158
Thorburns	42, 45
tourism	0, 2, 8, 11, 54, 55, 108, 178
traffic	69, 103, 131
trainees	54, 55
travelling exhibition	160
Treasury	39, 76, 197
trophy building	25, 169
troublemakers	121
truncheon	70, 88, 113
truncheons	8
types of visitor	21, 53

U

ultra vires.	196
unique selling point	90
utilitarian	112, 118, 161

V

van dock	43, 176
Vardon	30
vegetables	106
victim support	46
victims	141, 145
Victorian	79, 82, 90, 103, 119, 147, 172, 183
video clips	90, 136, 142, 155
violence	98, 99, 146, 148
Virtual Museum	11, 61, 92, 95, 156, 157, 158
visitor attraction	7, 11, 12, 21, 23, 30, 35, 38, 83, 85, 98, 170, 179
visitor numbers	5, 16, 22, 24, 55, 108
Voice recognition	136
void contracts	193
volunteer help	23
Volunteers	154

W

walk-through	92, 118, 119
walk-throughs	92
warrant	113, 158
welcome	109
Wheeler	25, 169
whistle	88, 89, 113
whistles	84, 142
wire-tapping	148
witnesses	141
women	56, 77, 115, 118
writers	157

ISBN 1412086786-7